Editorial Project Manager
Lorin E. Klistoff, M.A.

Managing Editors
Karen Goldfluss, M.S. Ed.
Ina Levin, M.S. Ed.

Illustrator
Renée Christine Yates

Cover Artist
Barb Lorseyedi

Art Production Manager
Kevin Barnes

Imaging
James Edward Grace

Publisher
Mary D. Smith, M.S. Ed.

Dr. Fry's Reading Activities

Grades 1–2 **Full Color**

Author

Edward Fry, Ph.D.

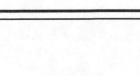

Teacher Created Resources, Inc.
6421 Industry Way
Westminster, CA 92683
www.teachercreated.com
ISBN-1-4206-3149-7
©2006 Teacher Created Resources, Inc.
Made in U.S.A.

P9-DEY-814

Table of Contents

Introduction

The full-color reading activities in this book are designed to reinforce reading skills. Classroom teachers, reading teachers, and special education teachers will all find these materials beneficial to their students. The activities can be used to supplement any reading program and other commerical materials. Many of the activities can be used in language arts centers. The materials and/or directions can be laminated so they can be reused.

The first part of this book contains activities that support phonics instruction. Students listen for the sound of blends and locate the letters on a bingo board. In another activity, students find the missing digraph using cards. One activity has students looking at a picture and its beginning sound and asks them to find the correct phonogram.

The next part of the book focuses on Picture Nouns. One of the activities has students match the Picture Noun with its word. The next activity asks students to read sentences and figure out the missing Picture Noun. Students will enjoy creating their own sentences using the Picture Nouns and Instant Words cards.

The last part of the book reinforces Instant Words. Dr. Fry's Instant Word list comprises the most important words for reading and writing in the English language. It is absolutely impossible to read or write anything without knowing at least some of these words. This book contains activities for teaching Instant Words 51–150. Whether through a pairs card game or a board game, students will learn the Instant Words that compose a high percentage of all reading material.

Students also can use the Picture Nouns and Instant Words Charts located at the end of the book to help support the activities included in this book.

For more practice with Dr. Fry materials, you can refer to two other full-color companion books which cover the other Instant Words and Picture Nouns. TCR 3148: *Dr. Fry's Reading Activities* (Grades K–1) covers Instant Words 1–50 and TCR 3150: *Dr. Fry's Reading Activities* (Grades 2–3) covers Instant Words 151–300.

Blends Bingo

Skill
- Students will match beginning blend sounds with their written letters.

Grouping
- pairs
- small group
- whole group

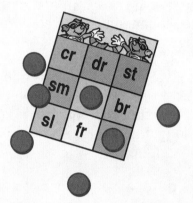

Materials
- Bingo Cards (pages 5–19)
- Blend Word Cards (pages 21–27)
- markers such as circular chips or pennies

Directions
1. Give each student a Bingo Card and some markers.
2. Cut out all Blend Word Cards and place them in a pile.
3. Have a student pick a Blend Word Card.
4. Have the student read the word on the card, emphasizing the beginning blend. (*Note:* You may want to ask the class to repeat the beginning after the student for more practice.)
5. Then, have all students check to see if they have the beginning blend on their Bingo Cards. For instance, if the word *spoon* was read, then students would check to see if they have the letters *sp* on their bingo cards.
6. If the student has found the blend on his or her card, have him or her place a marker on the square. Make sure to specify to students what determines a winner. (For example, chips that go diagonally, up or down, across, or "Blackout" where the entire board must be covered.)
7. Then, have another student pick a Blend Word Card and repeat the process again. Make sure all students get a chance to read the word cards.

Suggestions
- Laminate cards for durability.
- Have students create more word cards that contain blends at the beginning of the words.
- Challenge students by having them make a sentence that includes words from the Blend Word Cards, such as the following: The <u>green</u> <u>frog</u> was really a <u>prince</u>.

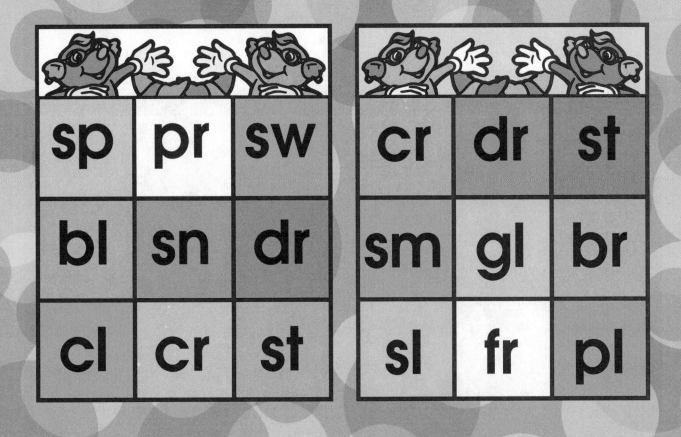

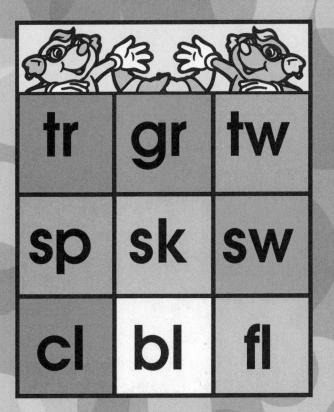

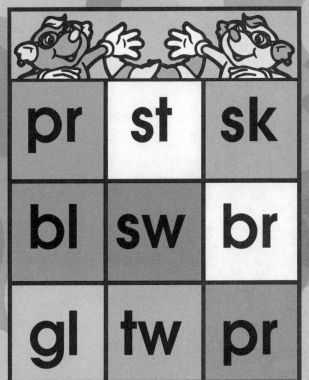

6

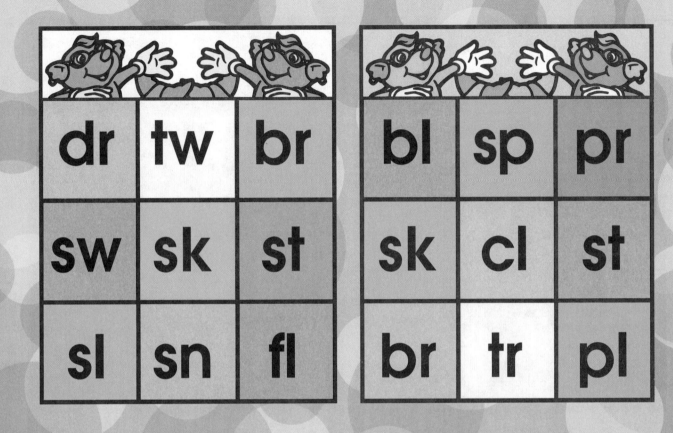

dr	tw	br
sw	sk	st
sl	sn	fl

bl	sp	pr
sk	cl	st
br	tr	pl

sk	fr	pl
bl	st	sm
cr	gr	sp

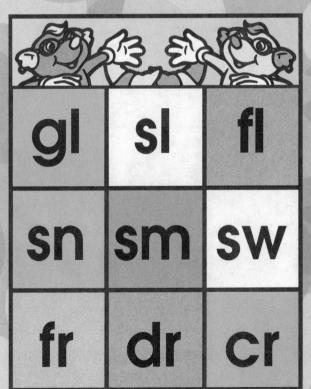

gl	sl	fl
sn	sm	sw
fr	dr	cr

8

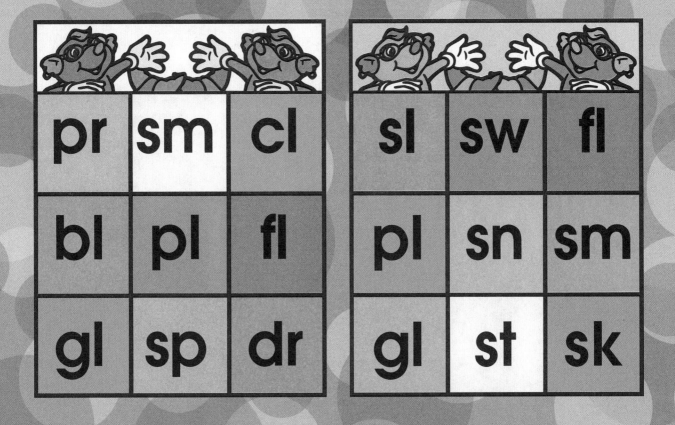

pr	sm	cl
bl	pl	fl
gl	sp	dr

sl	sw	fl
pl	sn	sm
gl	st	sk

fr	st	sk
bl	cl	br
tw	sp	pr

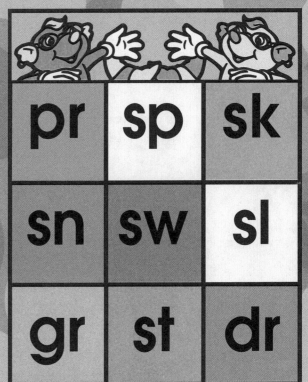

pr	sp	sk
sn	sw	sl
gr	st	dr

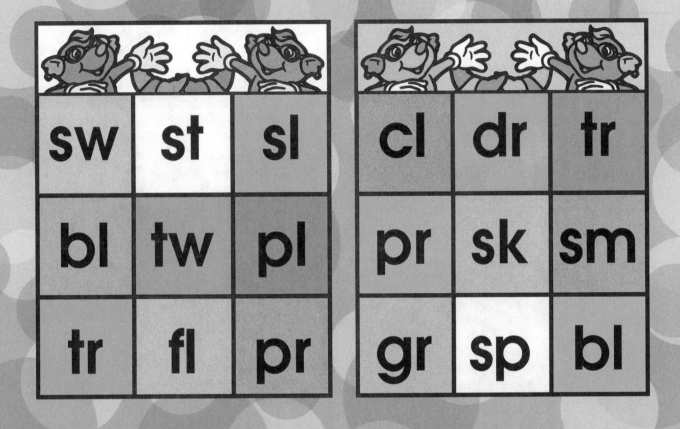

sw	st	sl
bl	tw	pl
tr	fl	pr

cl	dr	tr
pr	sk	sm
gr	sp	bl

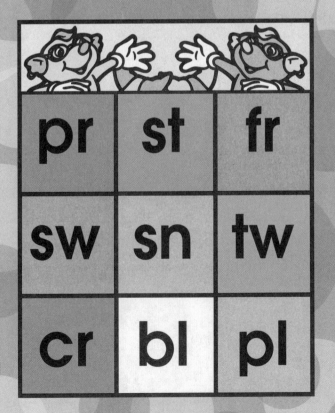

pr	st	fr
sw	sn	tw
cr	bl	pl

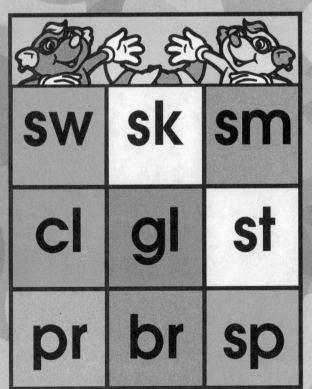

sw	sk	sm
cl	gl	st
pr	br	sp

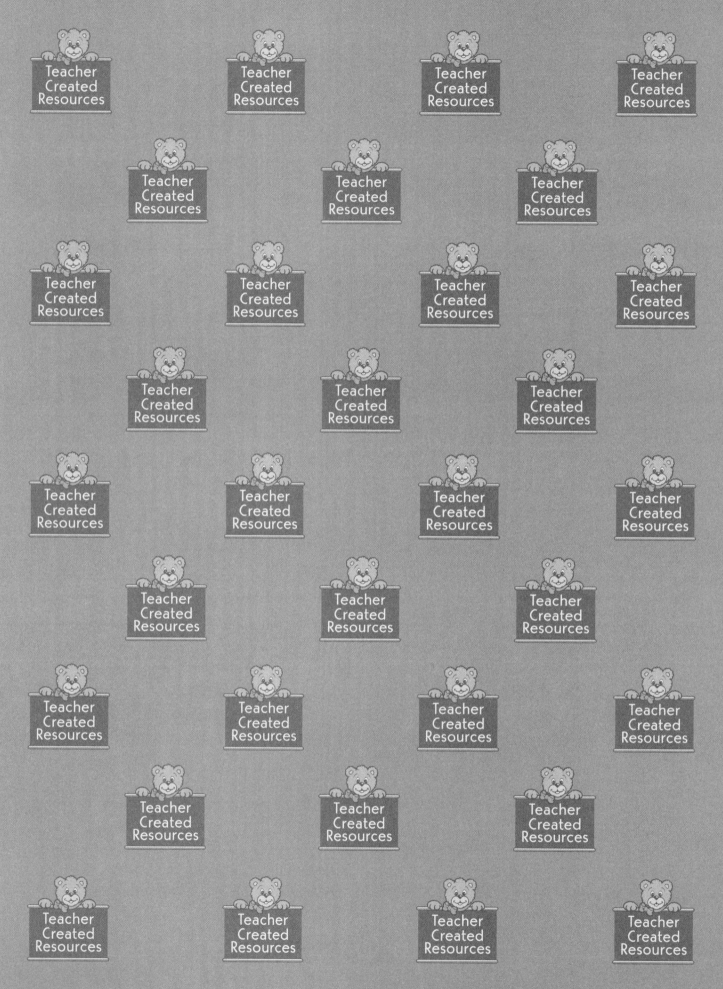

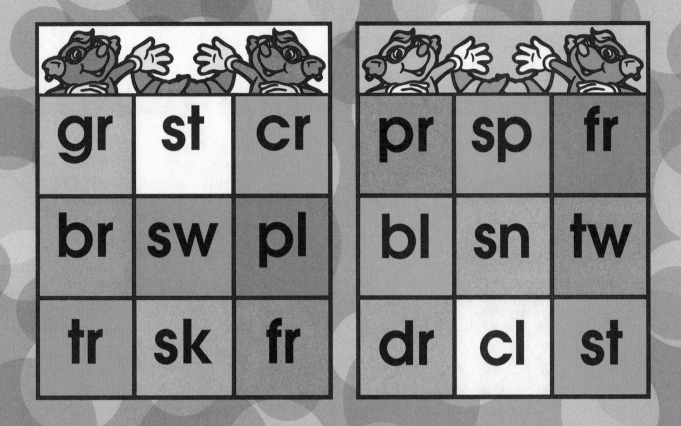

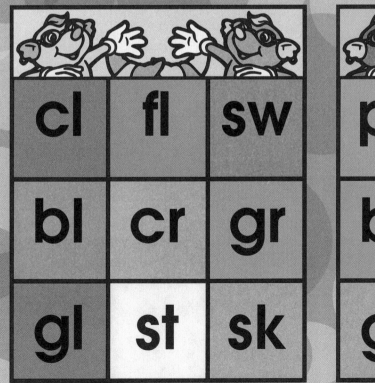

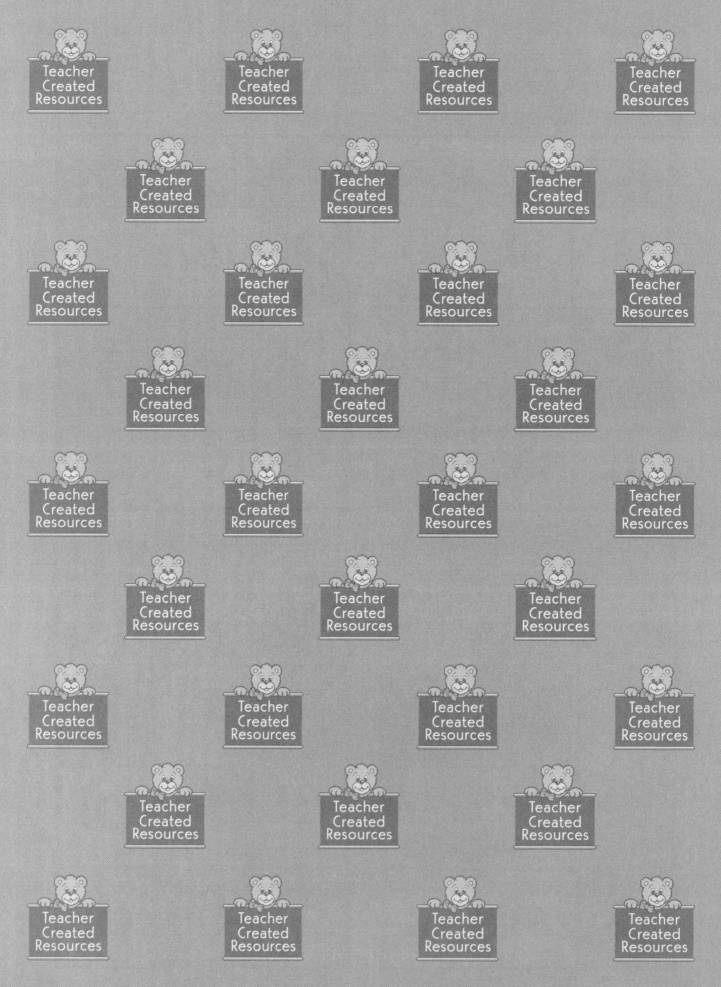

14

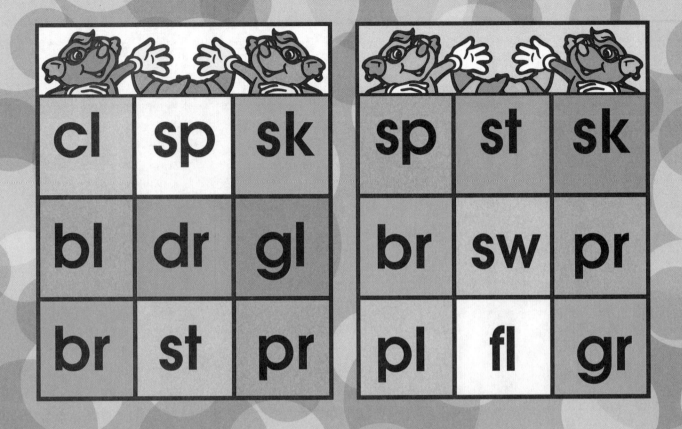

cl	sp	sk
bl	dr	gl
br	st	pr

sp	st	sk
br	sw	pr
pl	fl	gr

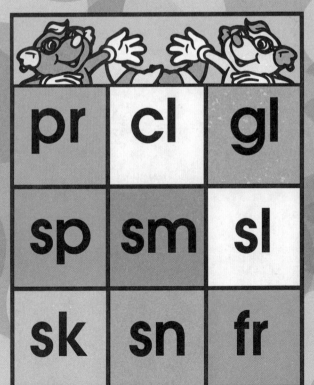

dr	pl	sm
bl	sn	br
tw	st	fr

pr	cl	gl
sp	sm	sl
sk	sn	fr

16

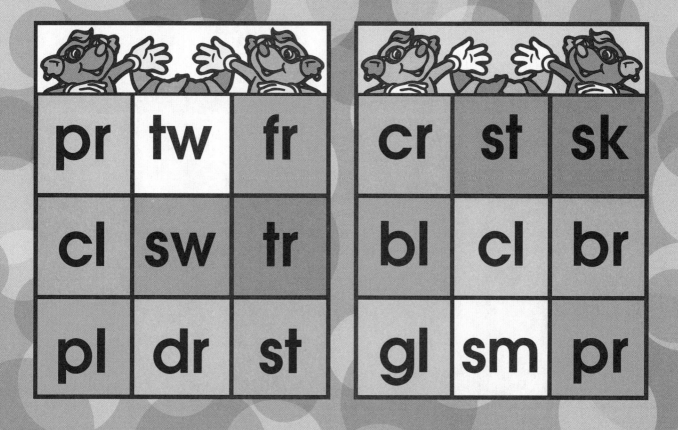

pr	tw	fr
cl	sw	tr
pl	dr	st

cr	st	sk
bl	cl	br
gl	sm	pr

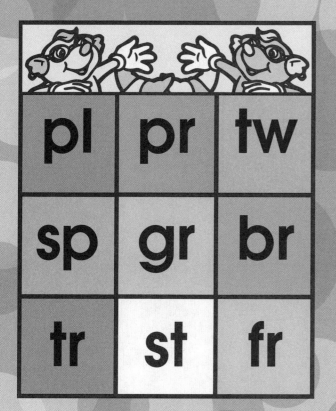

pl	pr	tw
sp	gr	br
tr	st	fr

pr	st	sk
fl	dr	sm
gl	sn	tr

18

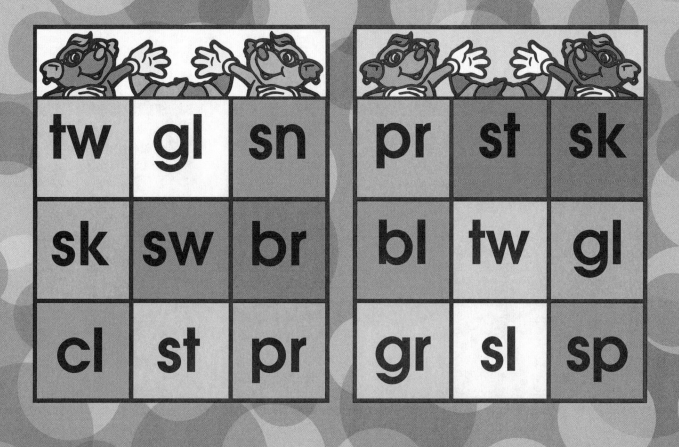

tw	gl	sn
sk	sw	br
cl	st	pr

pr	st	sk
bl	tw	gl
gr	sl	sp

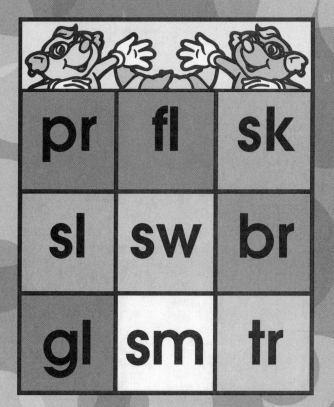

pr	fl	sk
sl	sw	br
gl	sm	tr

sp	br	sk
bl	sw	tr
sl	st	pr

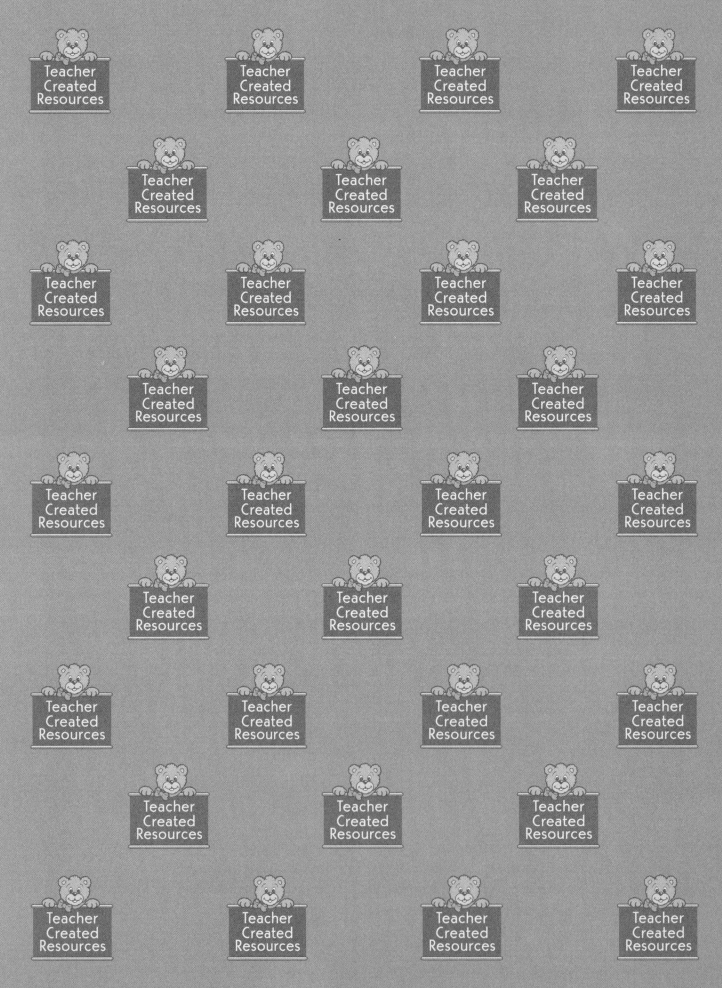

<u>bl</u>ack

<u>bl</u>ue

<u>cl</u>ock

<u>cl</u>own

<u>pl</u>ant

<u>pl</u>ane

<u>fl</u>ag

<u>fl</u>ower

<u>sl</u>ide

<u>sl</u>ed

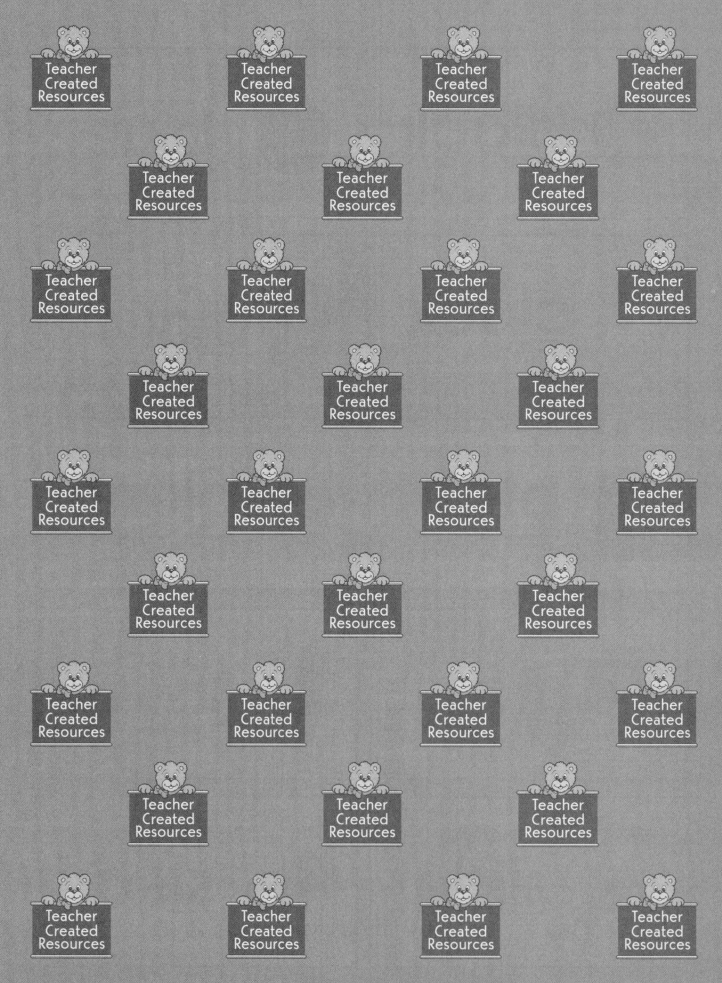

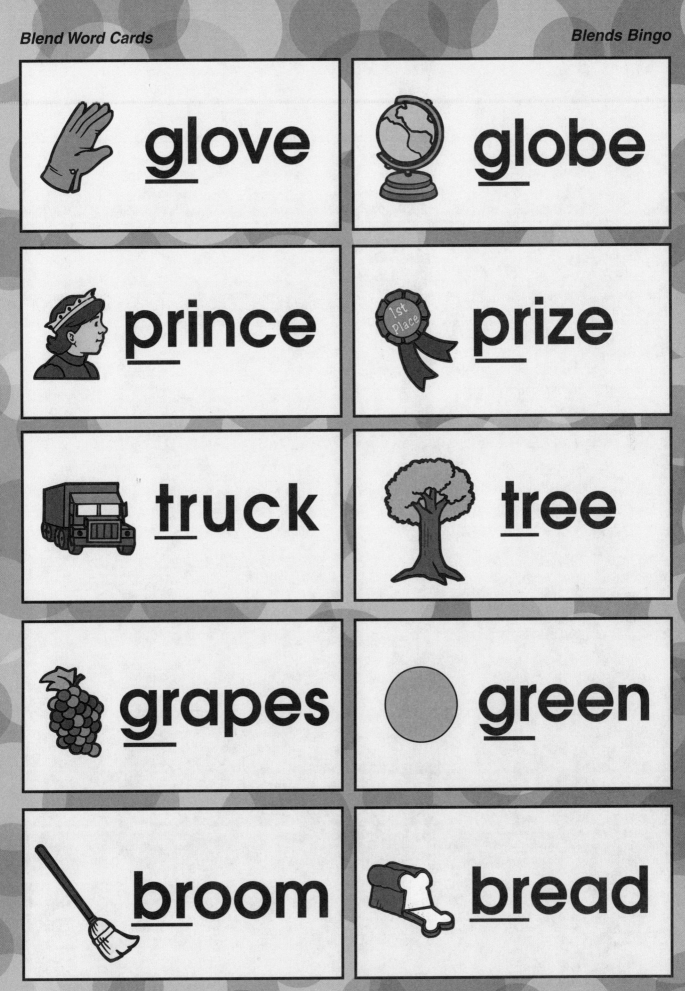

24

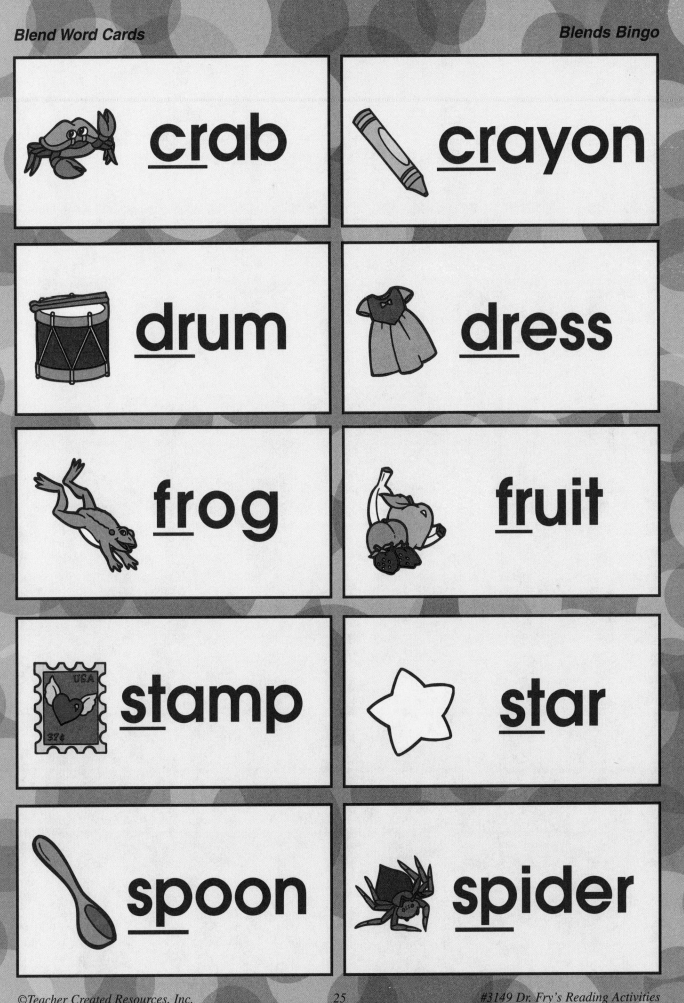

crab

crayon

drum

dress

frog

fruit

stamp

star

spoon

spider

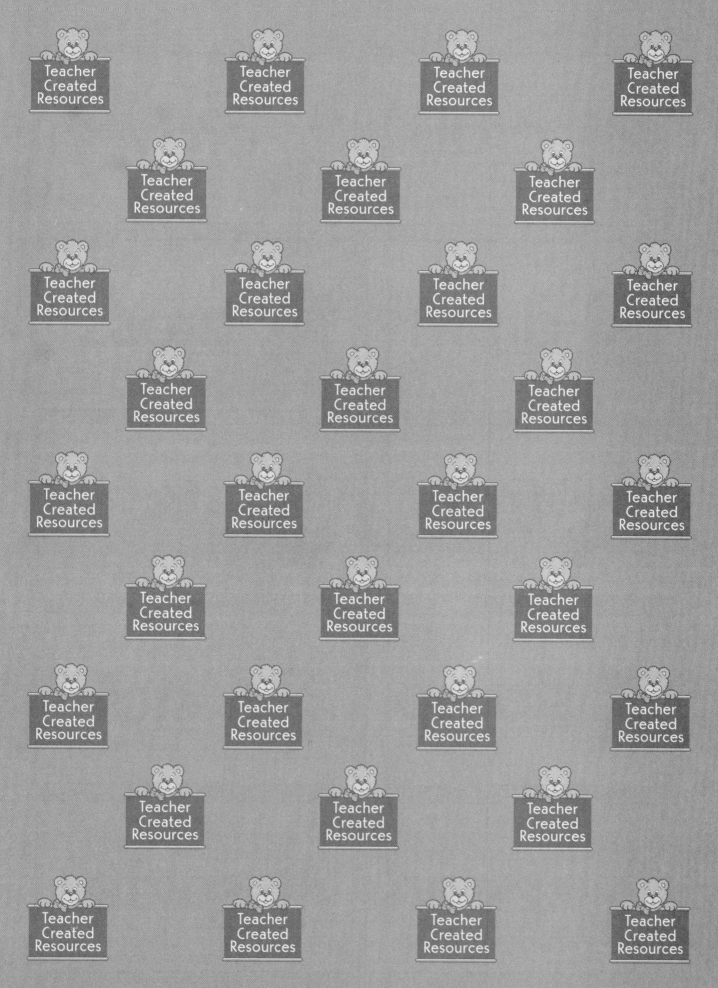

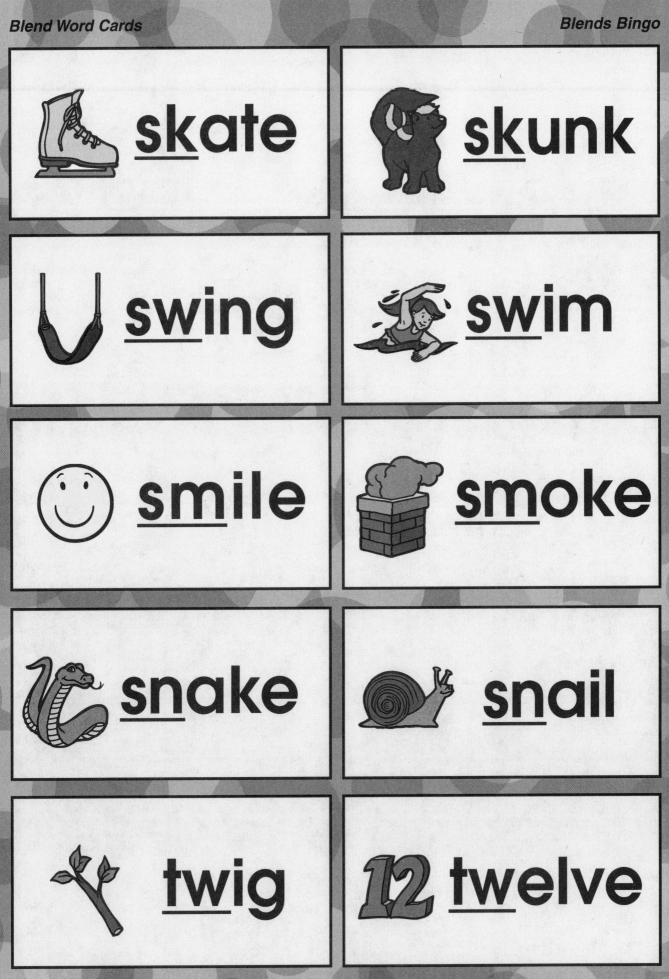

skate

skunk

swing

swim

smile

smoke

snake

snail

twig

twelve

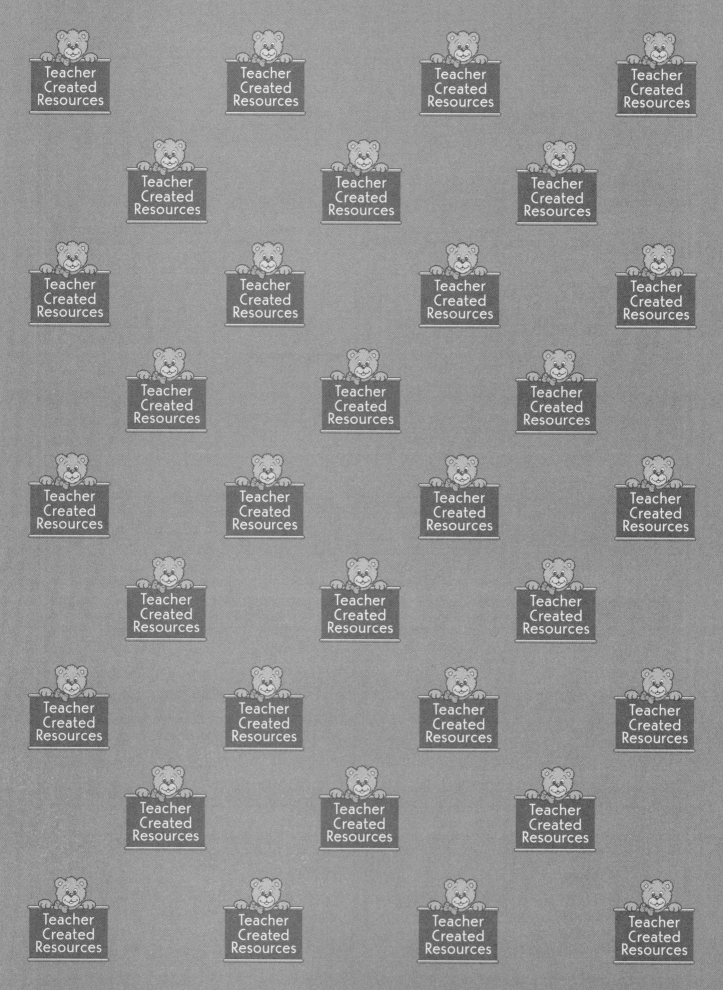

28

Missing a Digraph?

Skill
- Students will find the missing consonant digraph for each word.

Grouping
- independent
- pairs
- small group

Materials
- Digraph Cards (page 31)
- Picture Cards (pages 33–39)
- My Sentences (page 30)

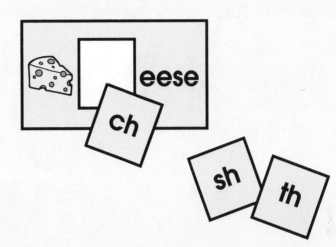

Directions
1. Cut apart and place all Digraph Cards face up on a flat surface so they can be seen by all students.
2. Cut apart and place all Picture Cards in a pile.
3. Have each student pick a Picture Card.
4. Have each student name the picture and the letters on the card.
5. Then, have each student try and find the missing digraph from one of the Digraph Cards that are face up.
6. When the student has found the missing digraph, have him or her place the cards together and read the whole word.
7. Have each student create a sentence for the word on the My Sentences recording sheet.
8. After he or she has recorded the sentence, have him or her read the sentence to a friend.
9. Next, have the student pick another Picture Card and repeat the process again.

Suggestions
- Laminate cards for durability.
- Blank cards are included on page 39 so students can create their own cards.
- Challenge students by having them make a sentence using more than one word that contains the same digraph. For example, I have <u>cheese</u> on my <u>cheek</u> and <u>chin</u>.

My Sentences

Name: _____   **Date:** _____

Directions: Record your sentences below.

1. _____

   _____

2. _____

   _____

3. _____

   _____

4. _____

   _____

5. _____

   _____

6. _____

   _____

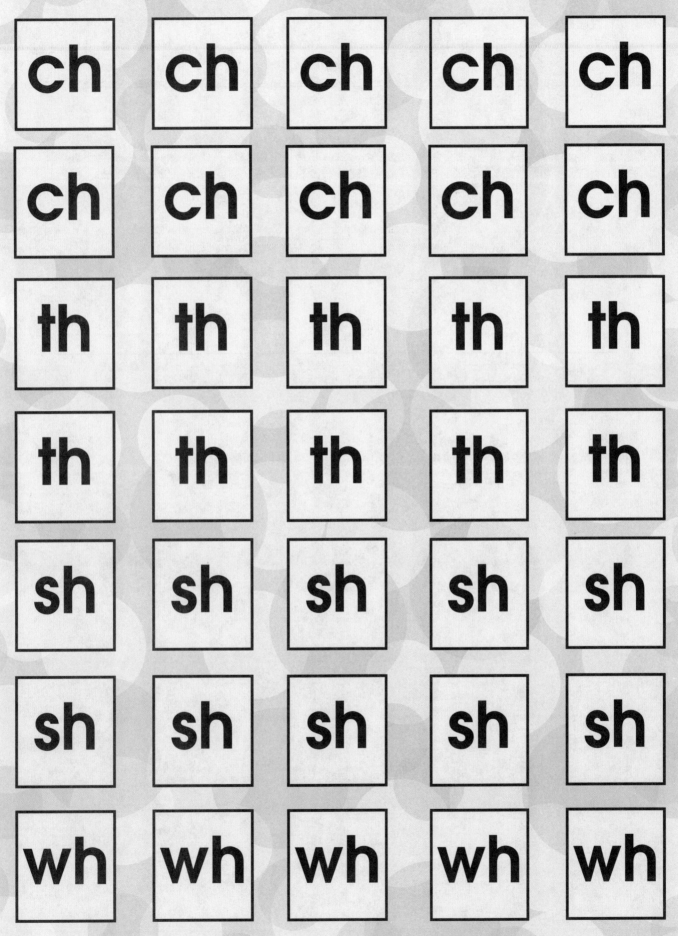

ch	ch	ch	ch	ch
ch	ch	ch	ch	ch
th	th	th	th	th
th	th	th	th	th
sh	sh	sh	sh	sh
sh	sh	sh	sh	sh
wh	wh	wh	wh	wh

eese

eek

in

ick

est

air

chur

eck

lun

wat

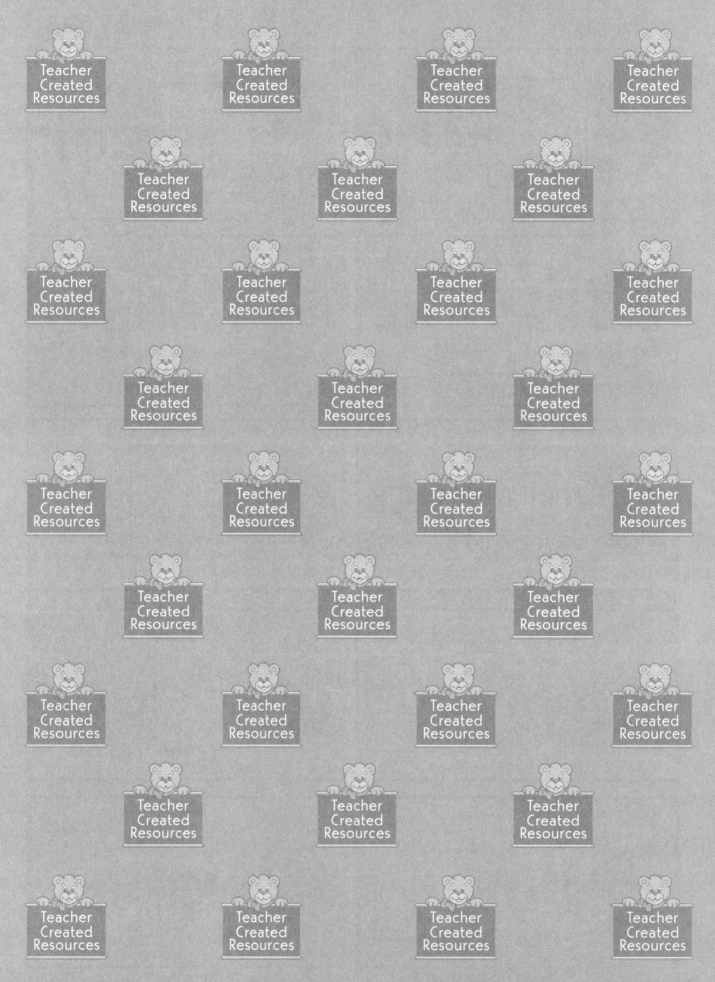

34

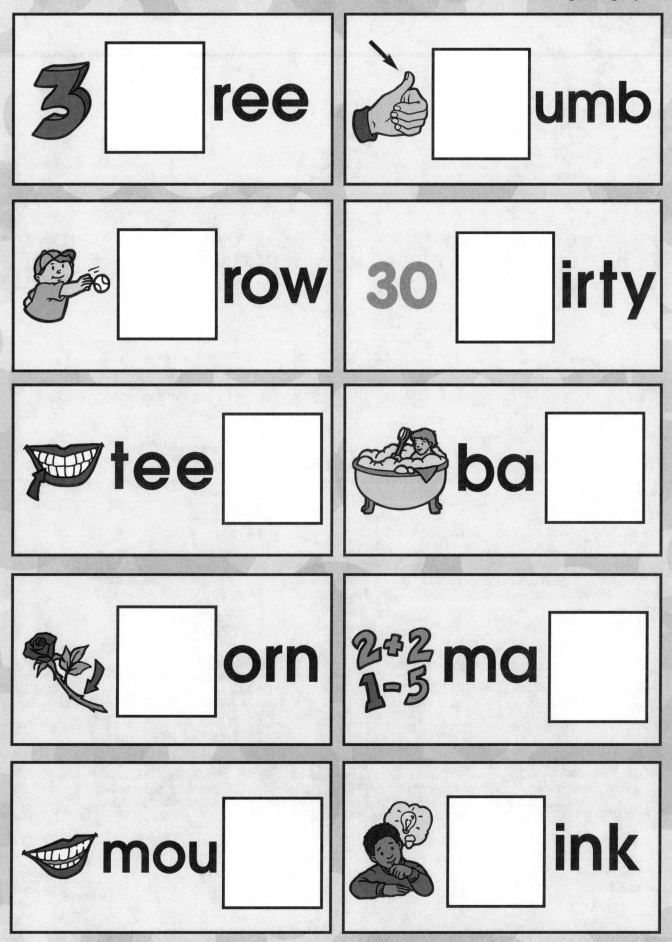

36

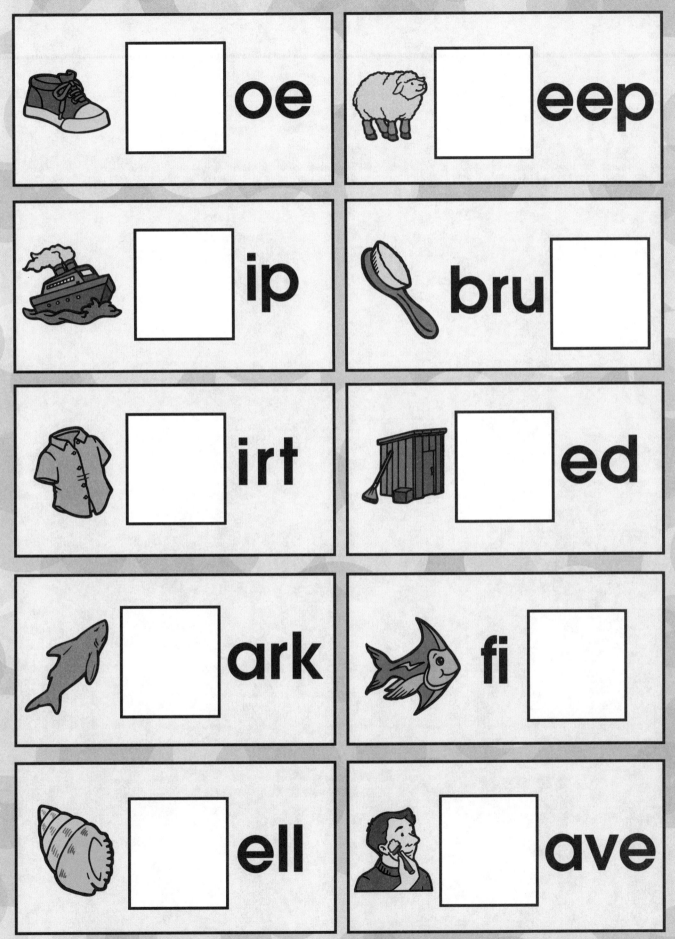

oe

eep

ip

bru□

irt

ed

ark

fi□

ell

ave

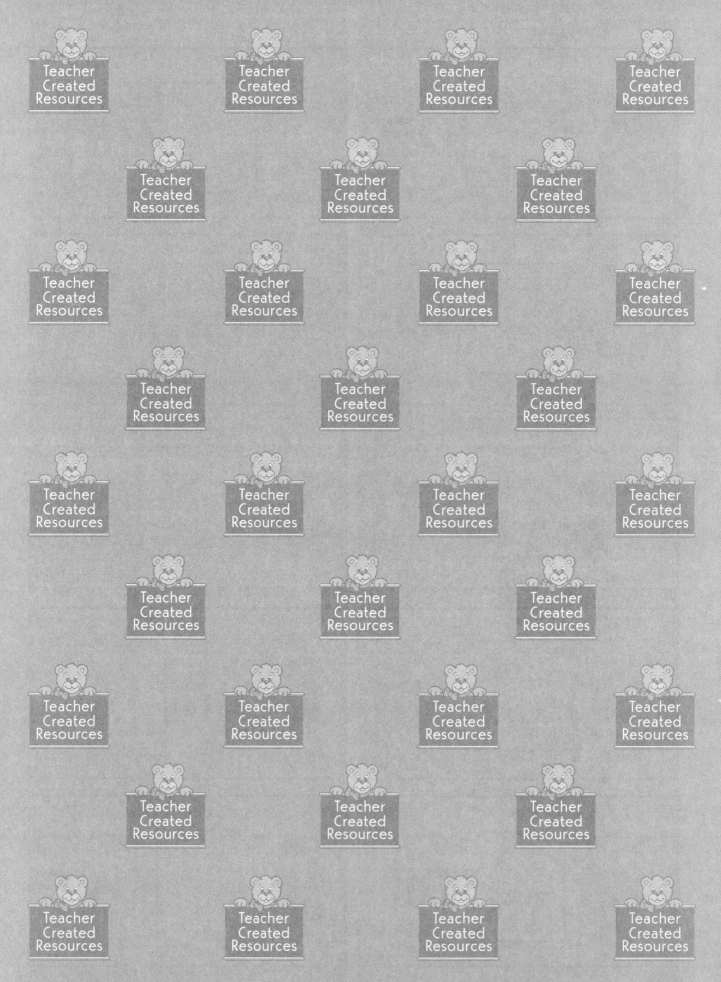

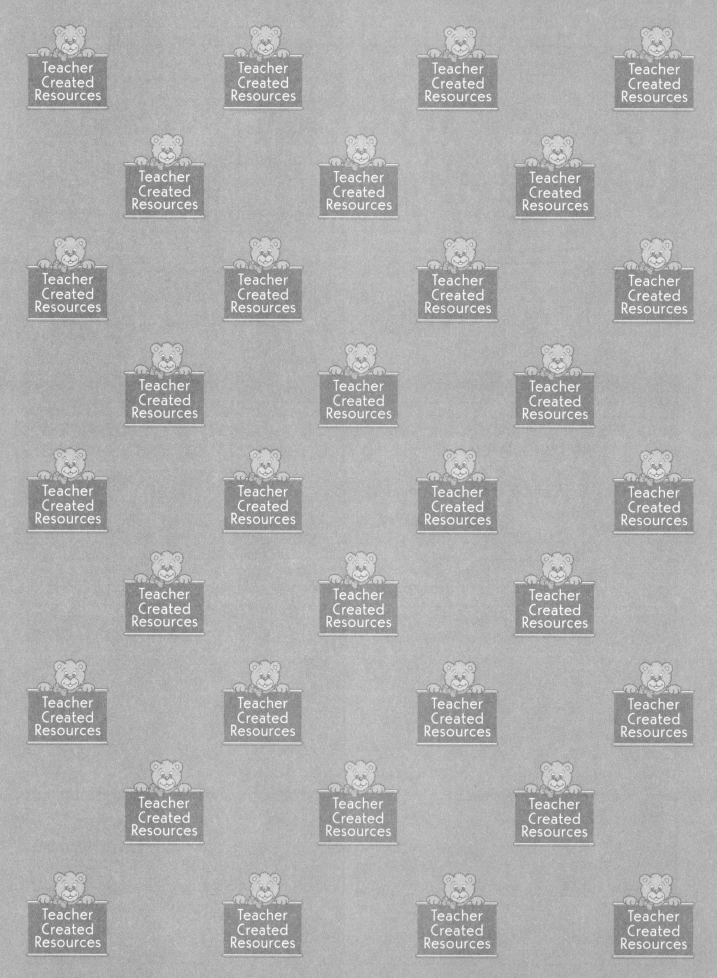

40

Find a Phonogram

Skill
- Students will match the beginning sounds of words with their phonograms.

Grouping
- independent
- pairs
- small group

Materials
- Phonogram Cards (pages 43–47)
- Beginning Sound Cards (pages 49–59)
- My Words recording sheet (page 42)

Directions
1. Cut apart and place all Phonogram Cards face up on a flat surface so they can be seen by all students.
2. Cut apart and place all Beginning Sound Cards in a pile.
3. Have each student pick a Beginning Sound Card.
4. Have each student name the picture and its beginning sound. (*Note:* A few beginning blends are included on some of the cards.)
5. Then, have each student try and find the matching phonogram from one of the Phonogram Cards that are face up.
6. When the student has found the match, have him or her place the cards together and read the whole word.
7. Have each student record the word on the My Words recording sheet.
8. After he or she has recorded the word, have him or her read the word again on the recording sheet—not using the picture on the cards but only reading the word on the paper.
9. Next, have the student pick another Beginning Sound Card and repeat the process again.

Suggestions
- Laminate cards for durability.
- When students have completed the activity above, have them make sentences out of the words on the recording sheet. For example, My black cat ate the ham.

My Words

Name: _____ **Date:** _____

1. _____   2. _____

3. _____   4. _____

5. _____   6. _____

7. _____   8. _____

9. _____   10. _____

11. _____   12. _____

13. _____   14. _____

15. _____   16. _____

17. _____   18. _____

19. _____   20. _____

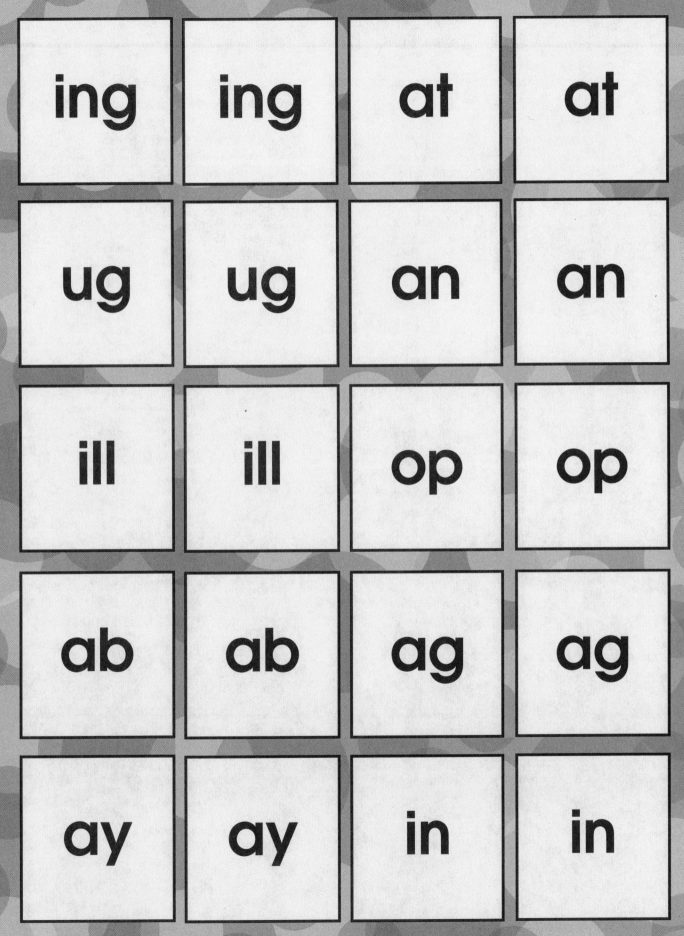

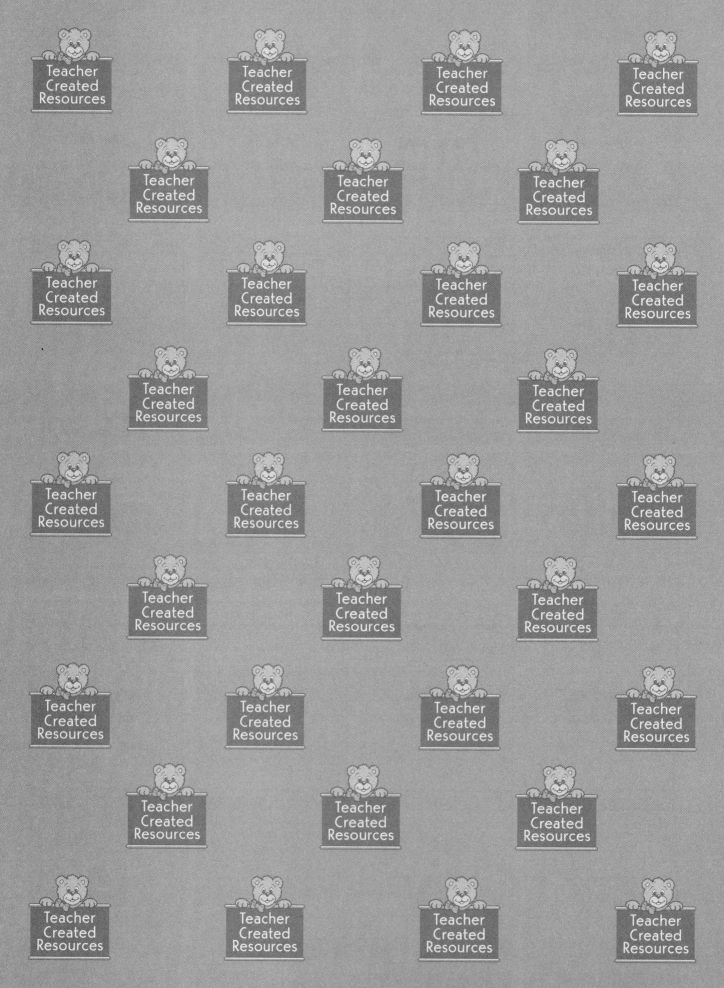

44

um	um	uck	uck
ine	ine	ake	ake
ock	ock	am	am
ot	ot	ail	ail
ink	ink	ain	ain

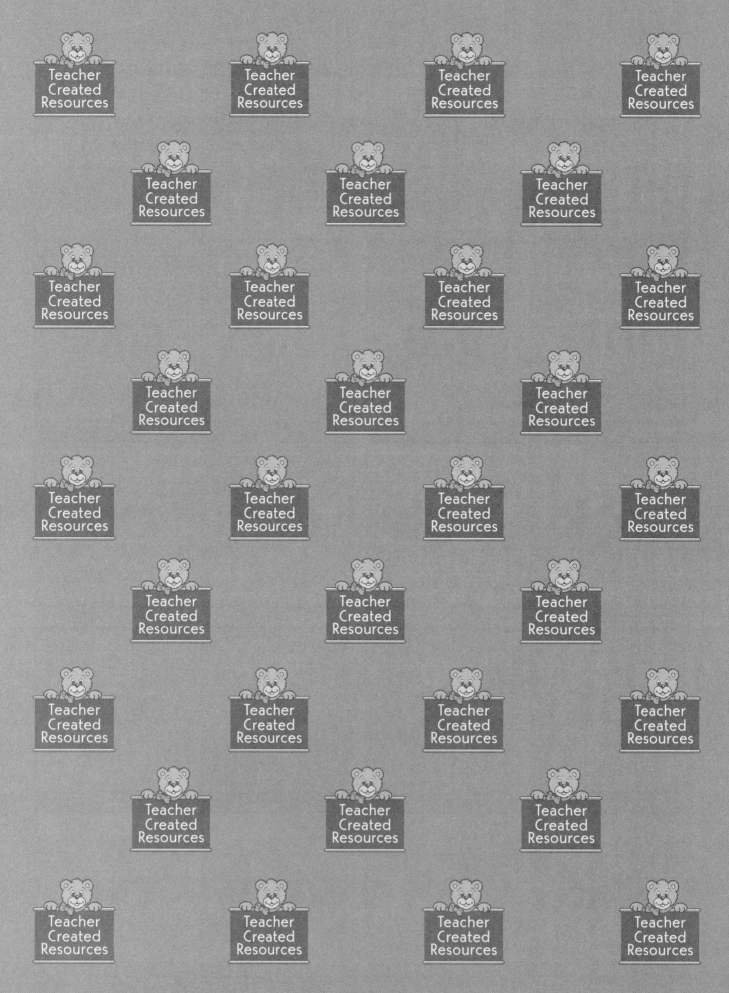

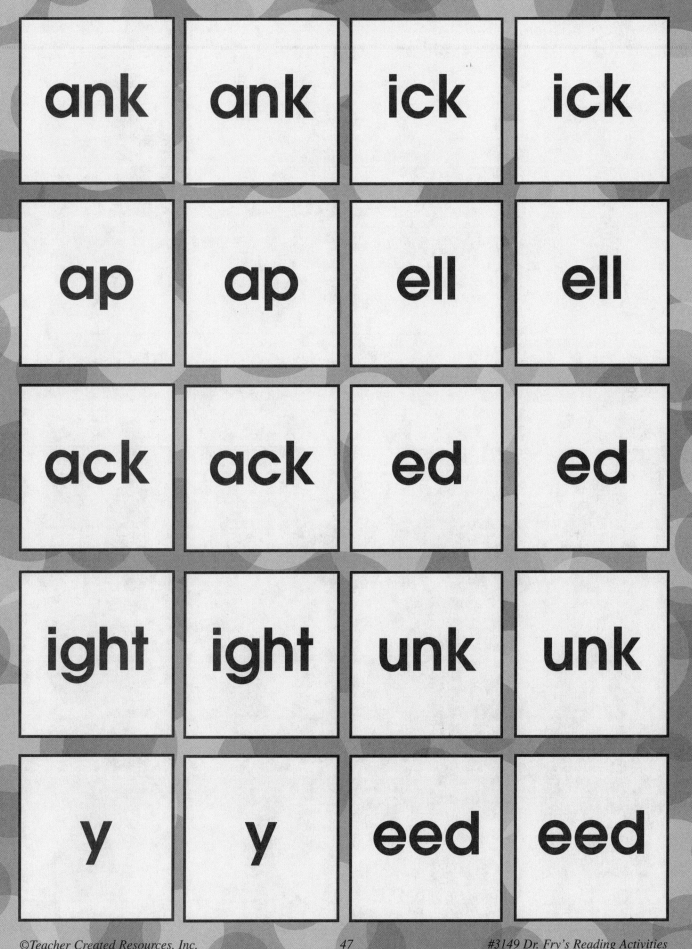

ank	ank	ick	ick
ap	ap	ell	ell
ack	ack	ed	ed
ight	ight	unk	unk
y	y	eed	eed

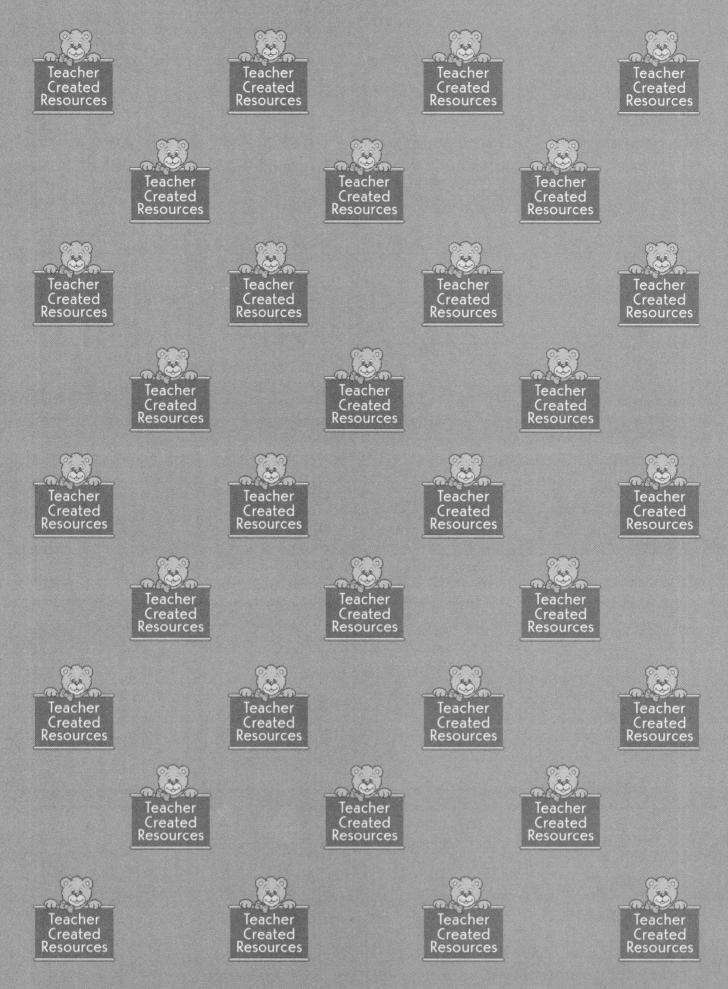

48

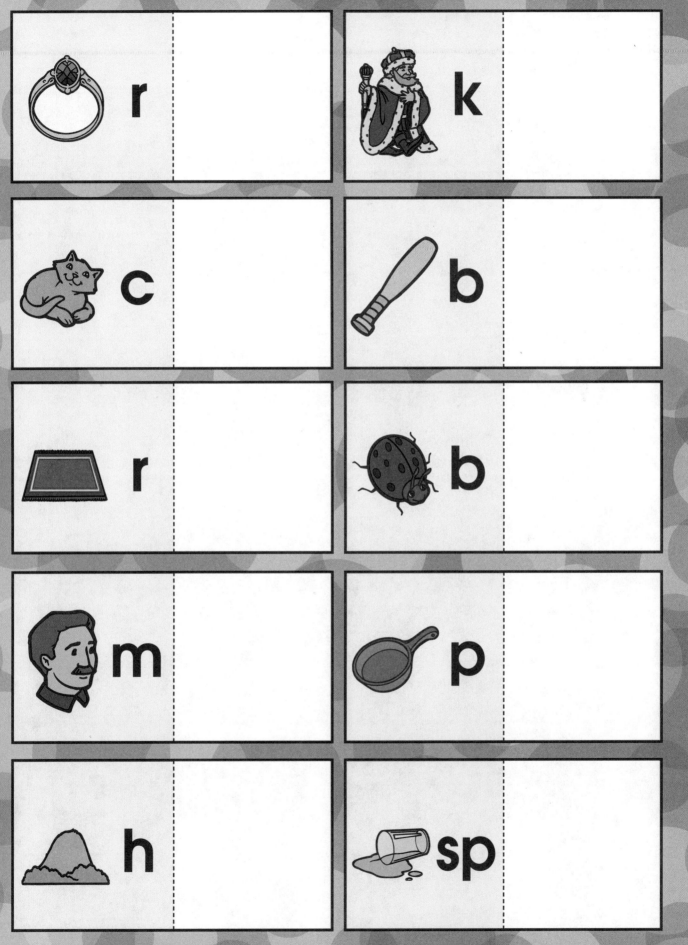

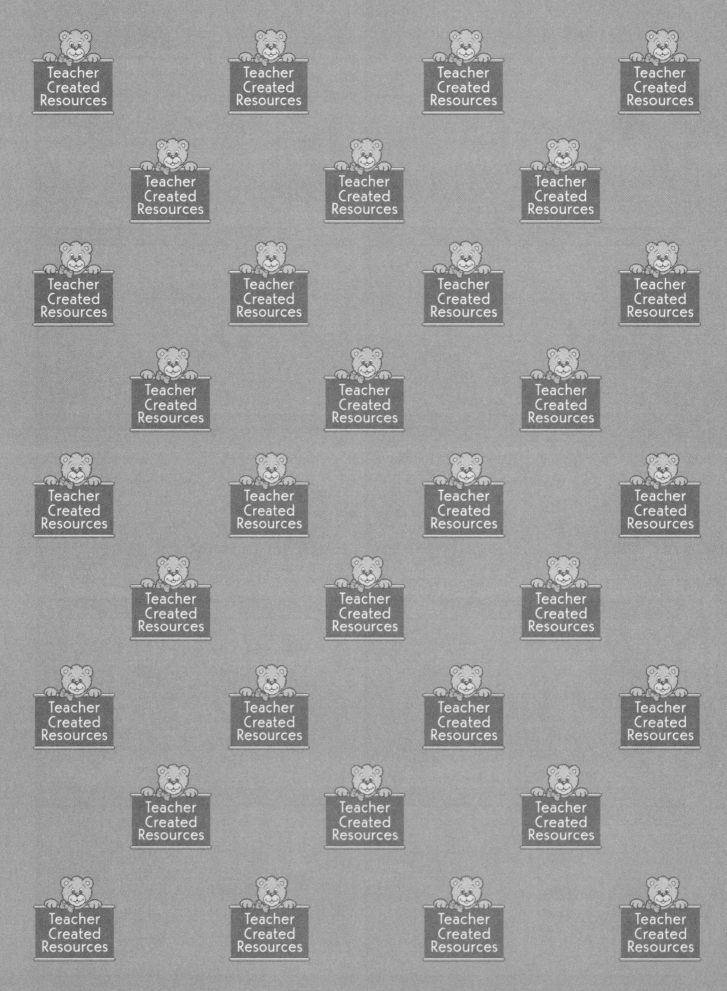

50

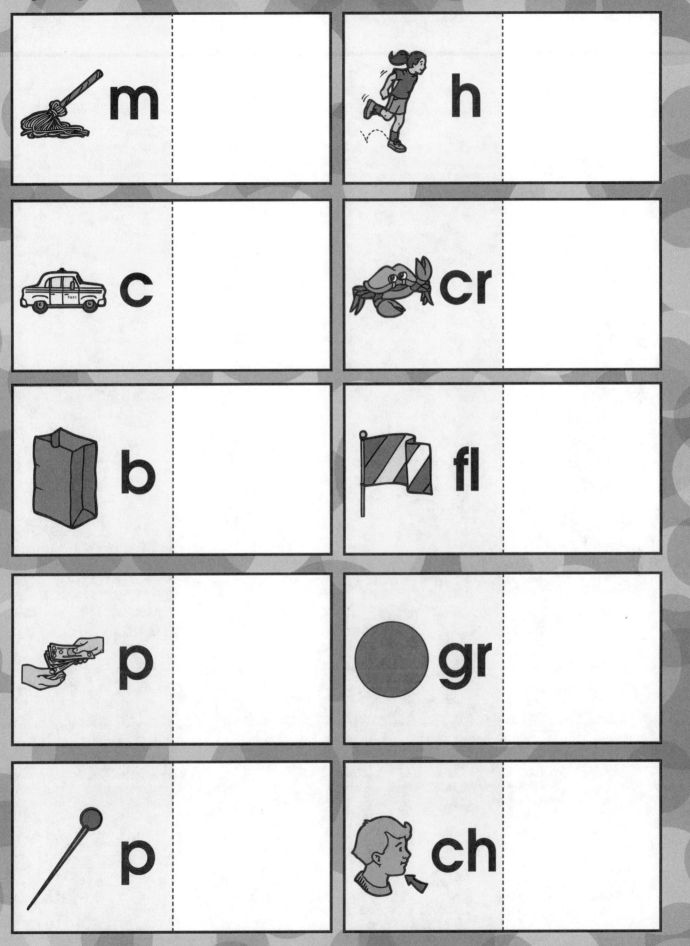

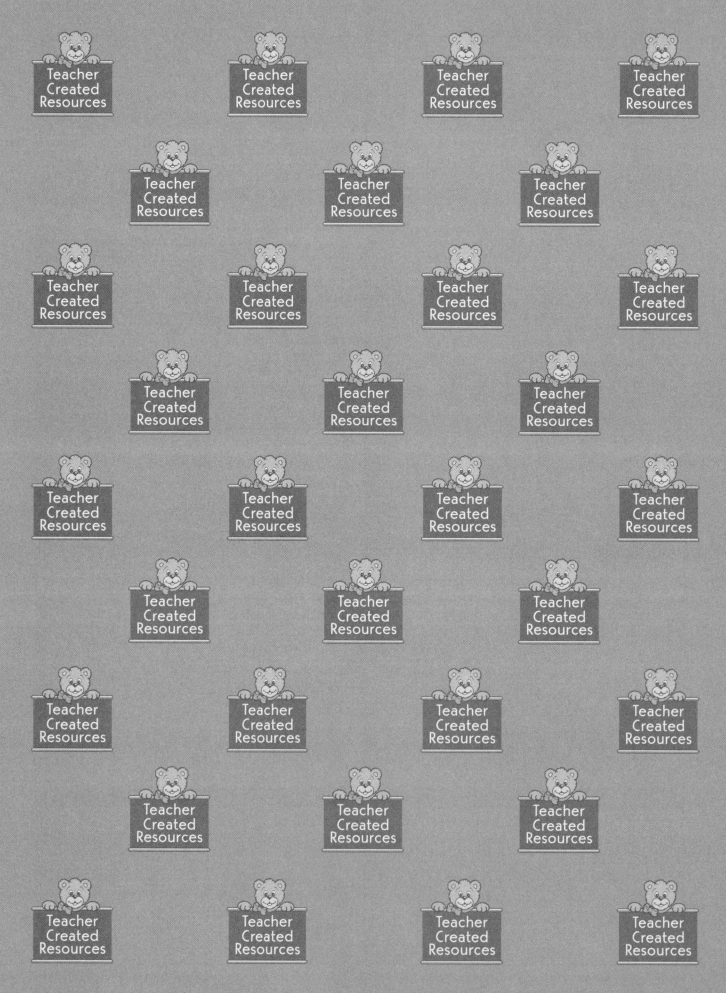

52

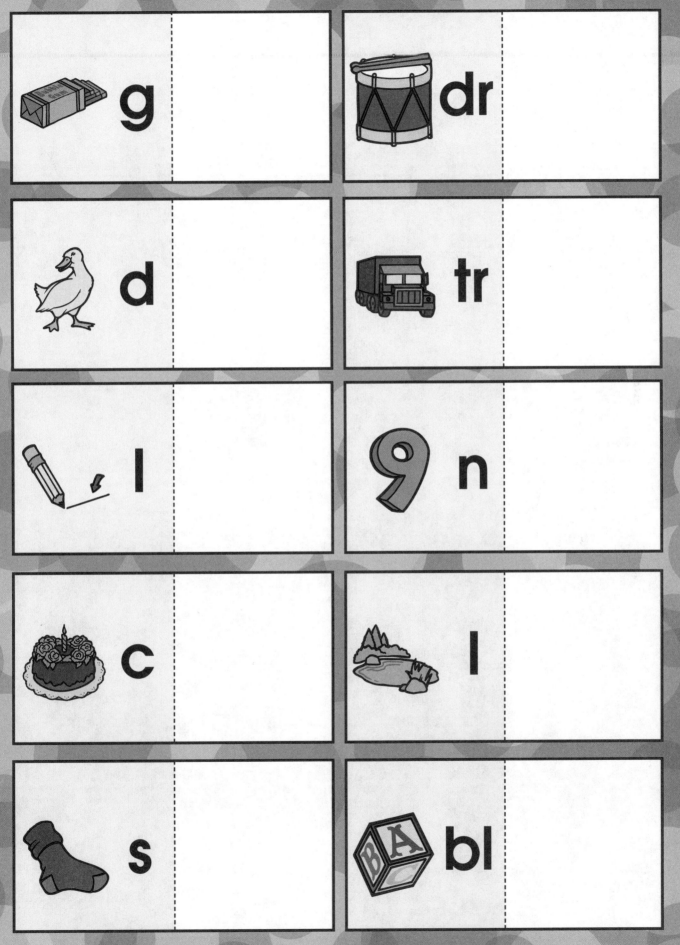

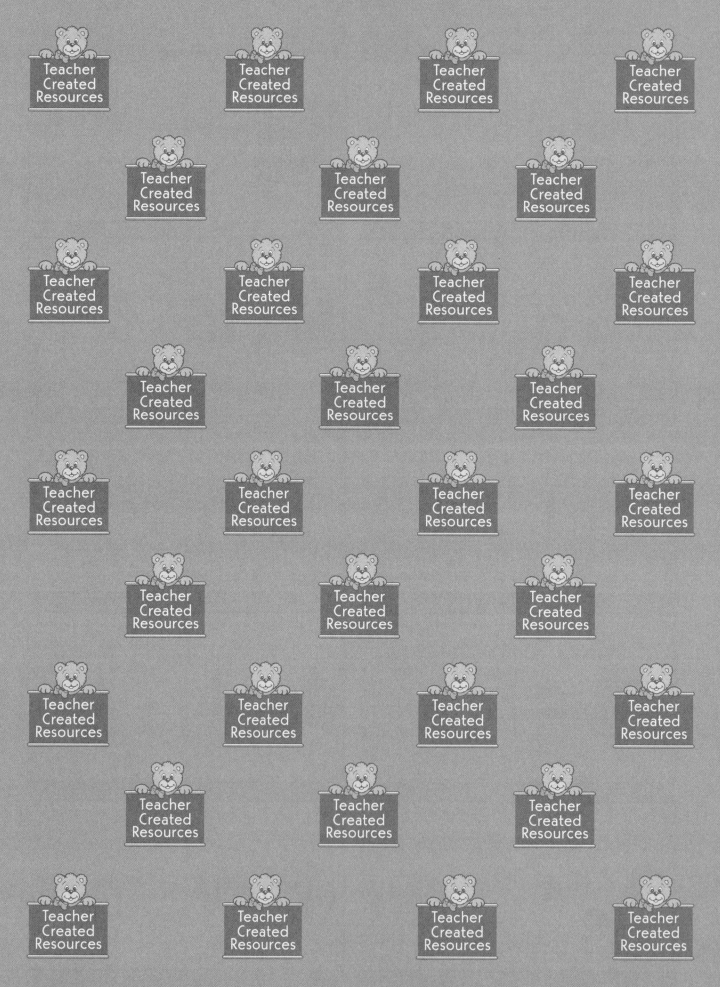

54

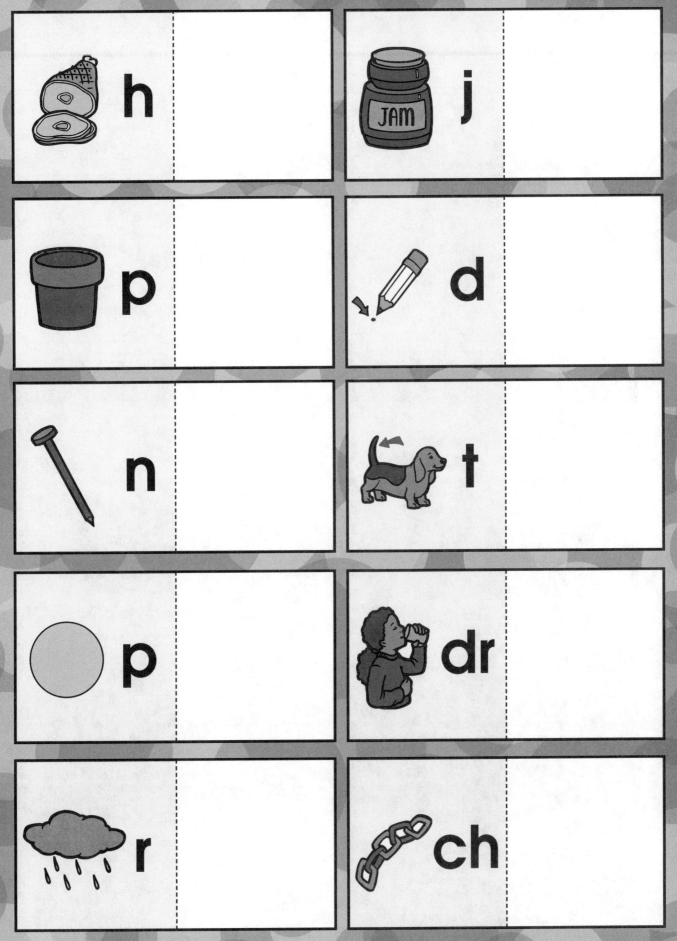

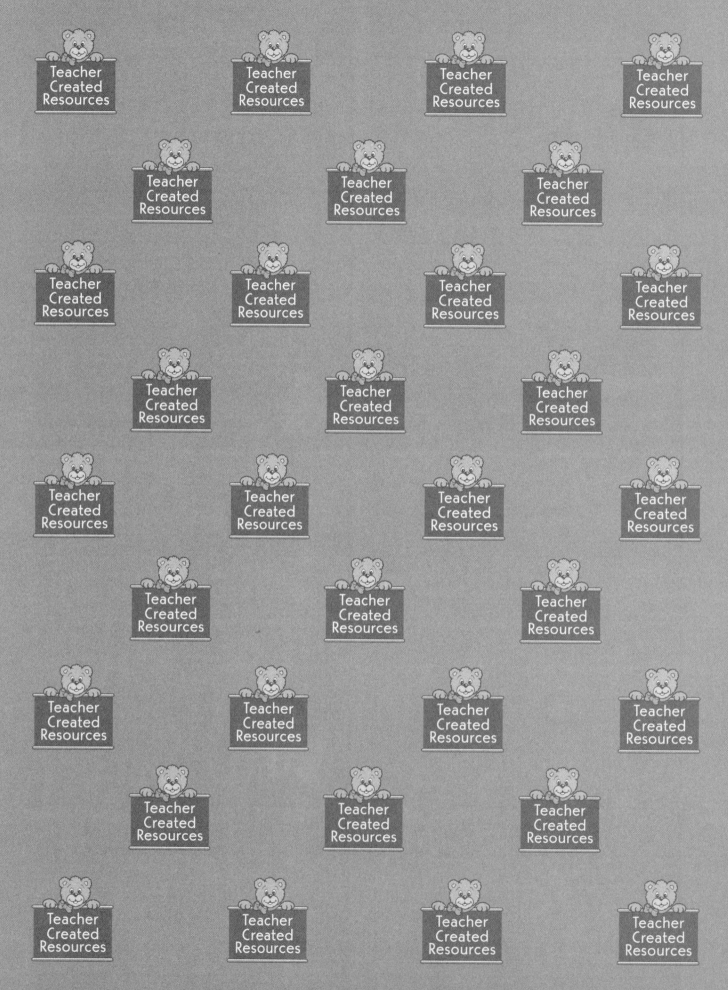

56

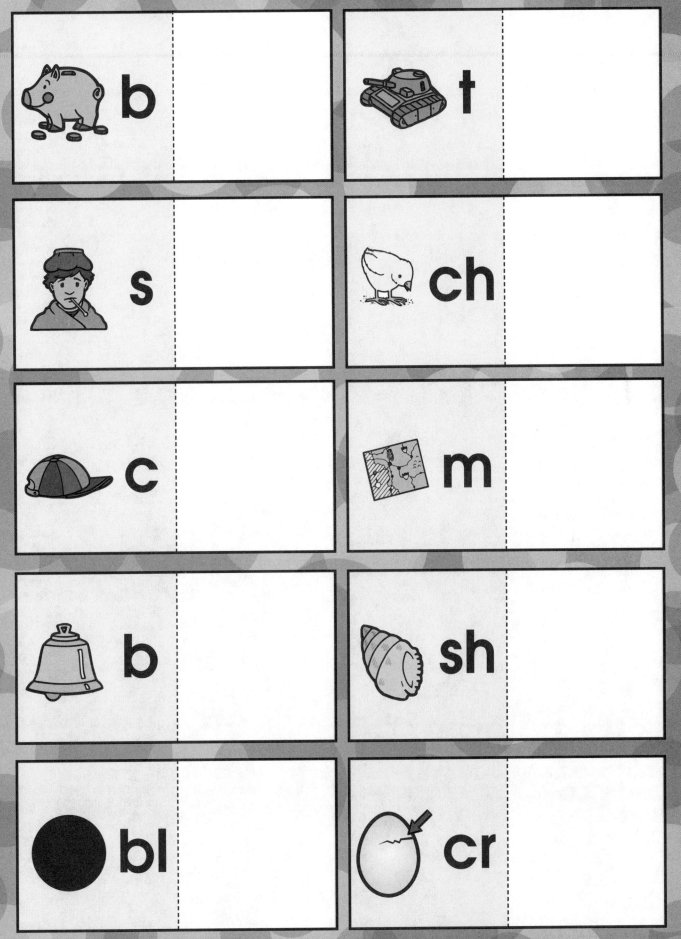

58

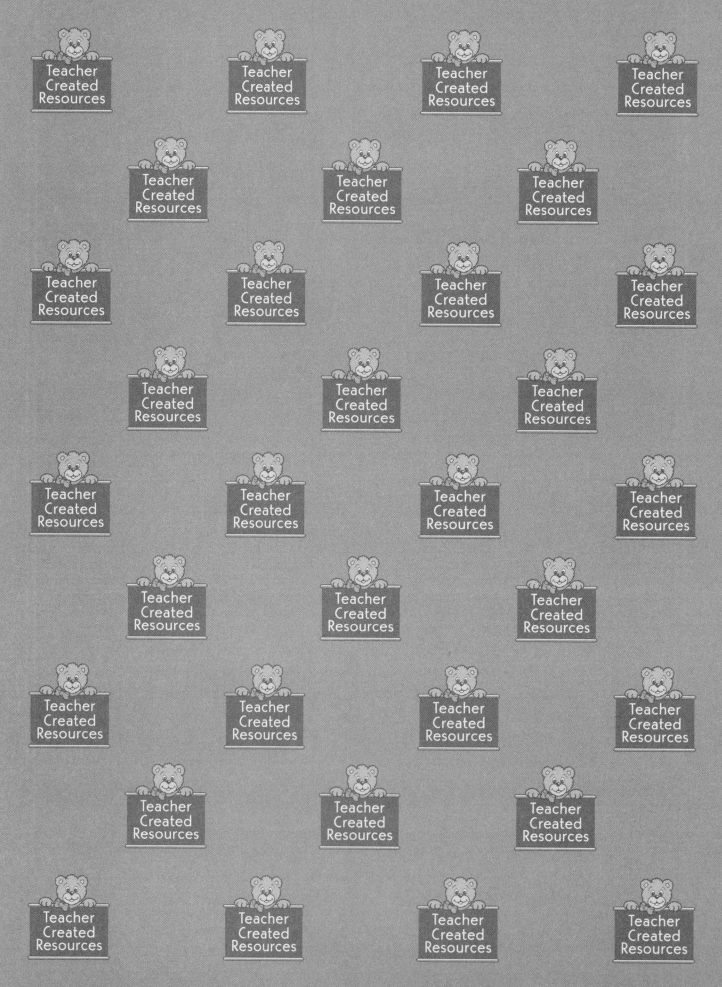

60

Picture Noun Match

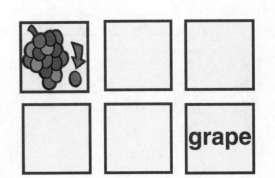

Skill
- Students will match Picture Nouns to their words.

Grouping
- independent
- pairs
- small group

Materials
- Picture Noun Cards (pages 63–71)
- Picture Noun Match recording sheet (page 62)

Directions
1. Cut apart and mix up the Picture Noun Cards (including word cards).
2. Spread all cards face down on a flat surface.
3. In turn, have each student flip two cards face up.
4. Have the student say the name of the picture and/or read the word. If the word matches with the picture, then the student keeps the match and gets another turn. If the word does not match the picture, then the cards are placed face down and the next person gets a turn.
5. Remind students that they must remember where cards are placed so on their next turn they can find a match.
6. Hand out a recording sheet to each student and have them record their matches.

Suggestions
- For beginning readers, start with just a few word and picture cards.
- Have students create their own picture noun cards using page 62. Have them draw a picture in the box on the left and write the word in the right box. To extend this activity further, have students create their own dictionaries from paper. Have them write one letter per piece of paper and staple all 26 papers together. Then, have them glue their picture nouns inside according to the beginning letter.
- Have students categorize the picture cards or word cards using the sorting charts on pages 73 and 75.
- Use the Picture Cards with the activity on page 77.
- Have students write sentences which include their Picture Nouns.
- Have students use the charts on pages 171 and 173 to check their answers to the Picture Noun Match.

Picture Noun Match

Name: _____

Date: _____

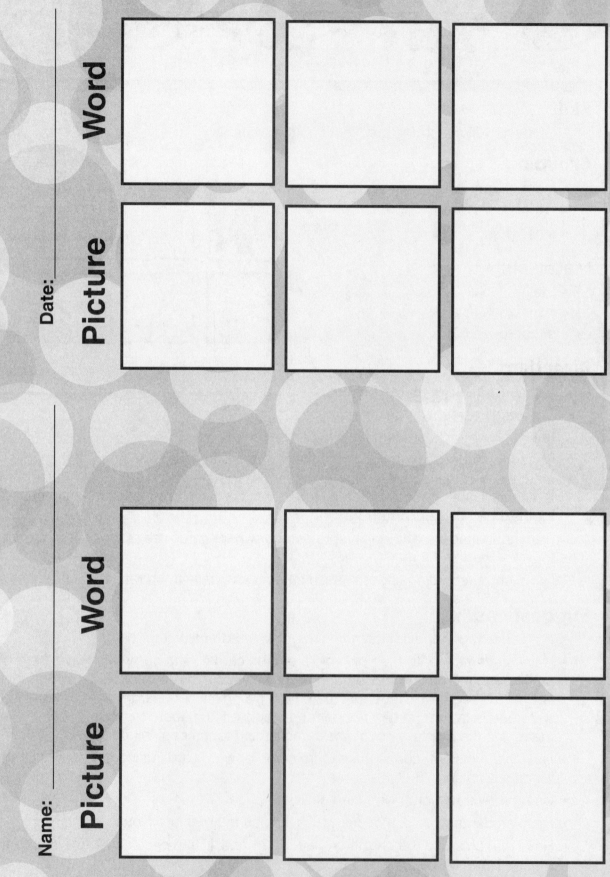

Word	Picture

Word	Picture

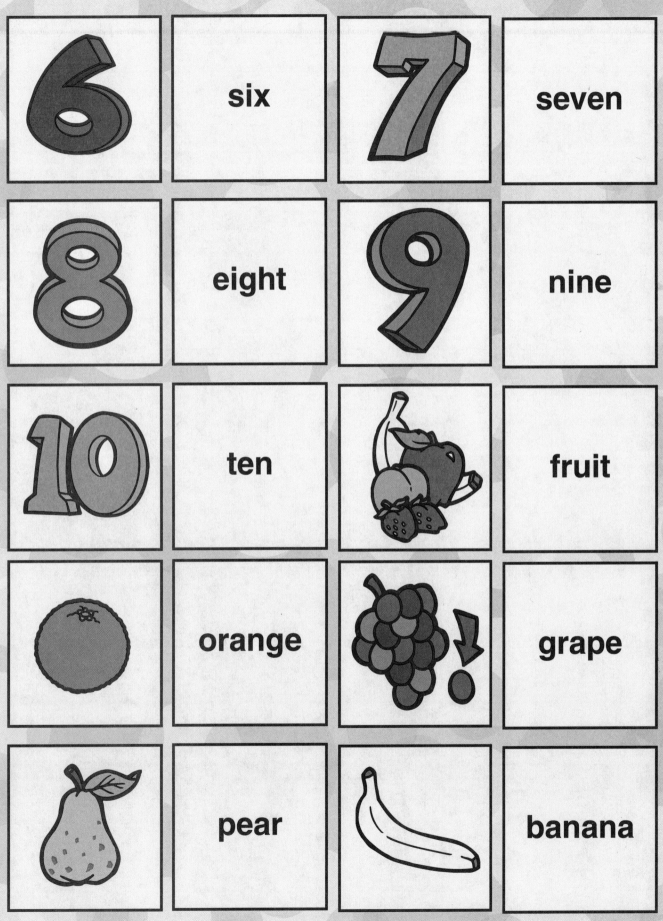

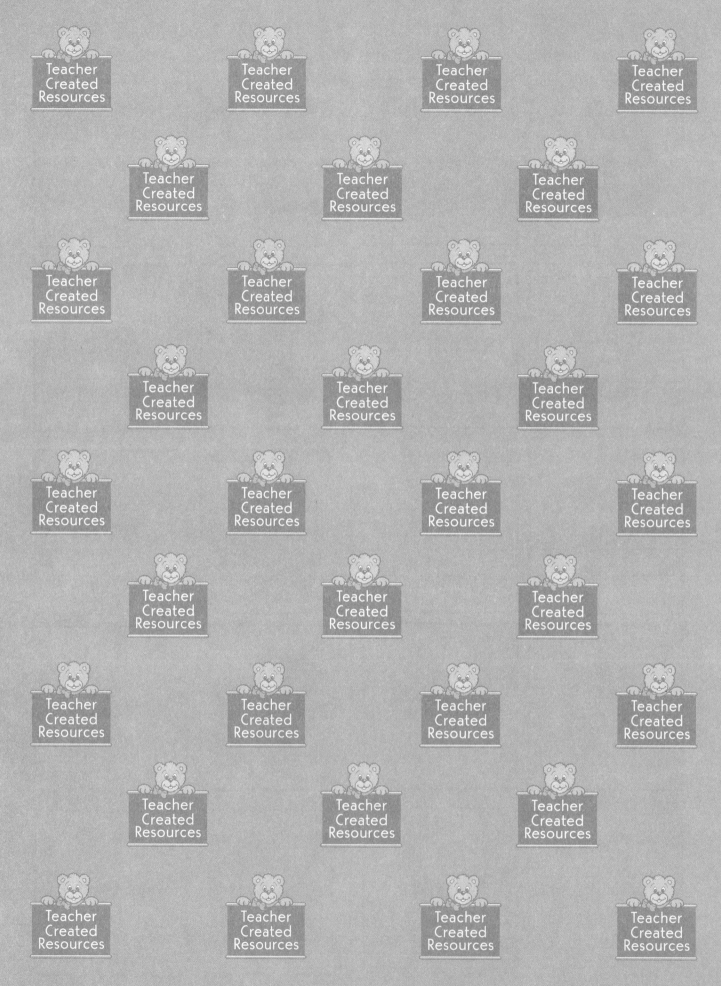

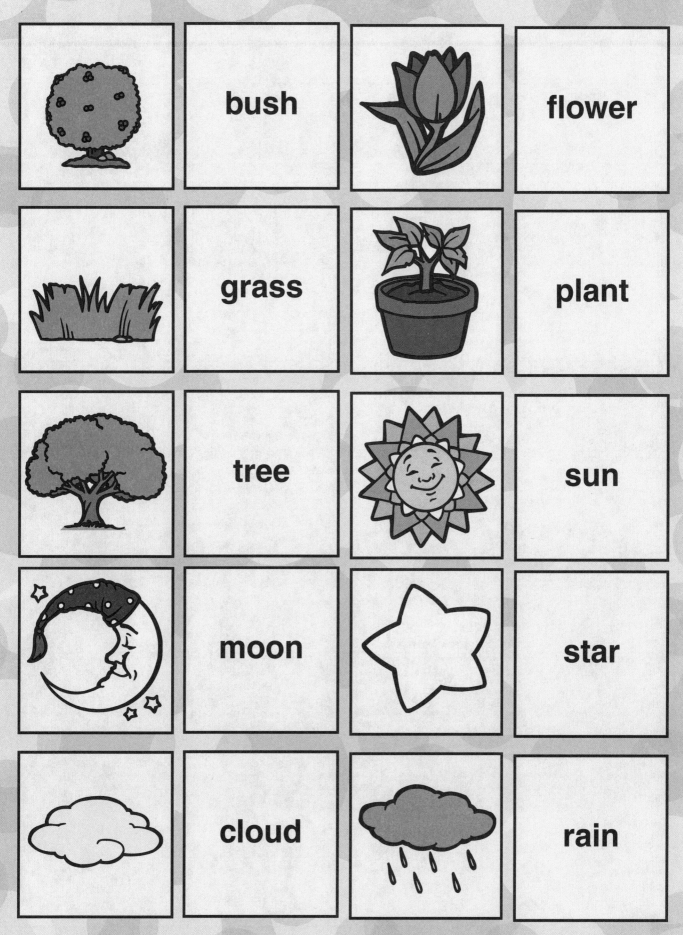

	bush		flower
	grass		plant
	tree		sun
	moon		star
	cloud		rain

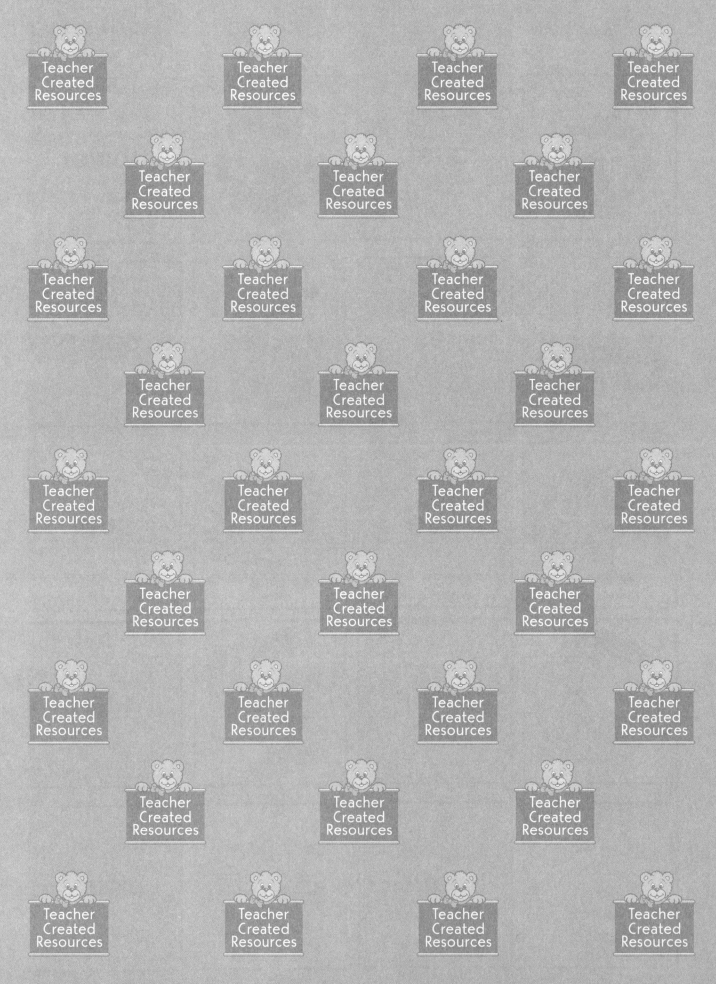

66

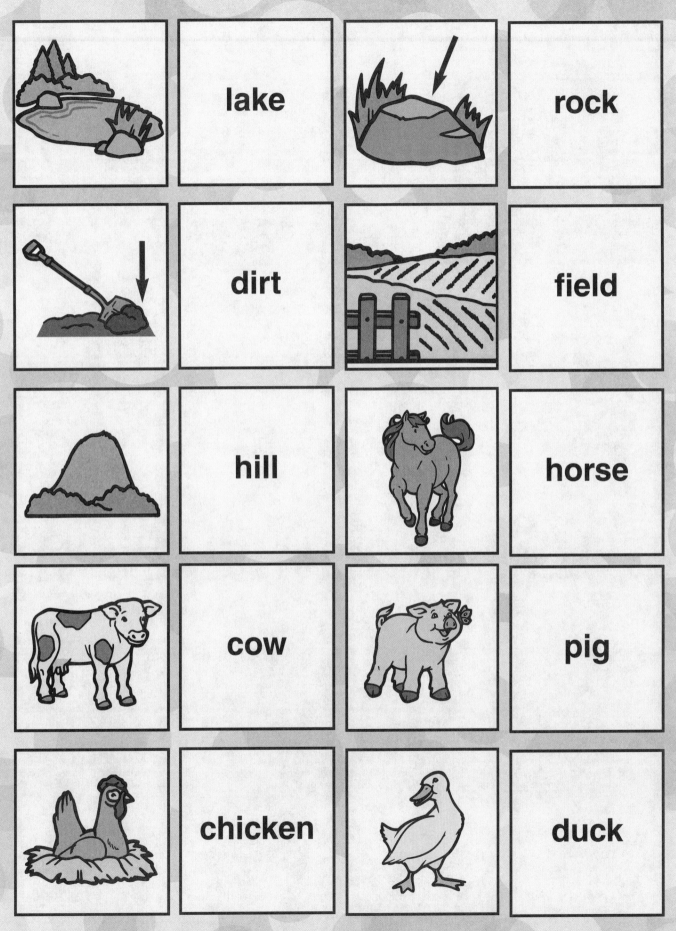

	lake		rock
dirt			field
	hill		horse
	cow		pig
	chicken		duck

farmer

policeman

cook

doctor

nurse

television

radio

movie

ball game

band

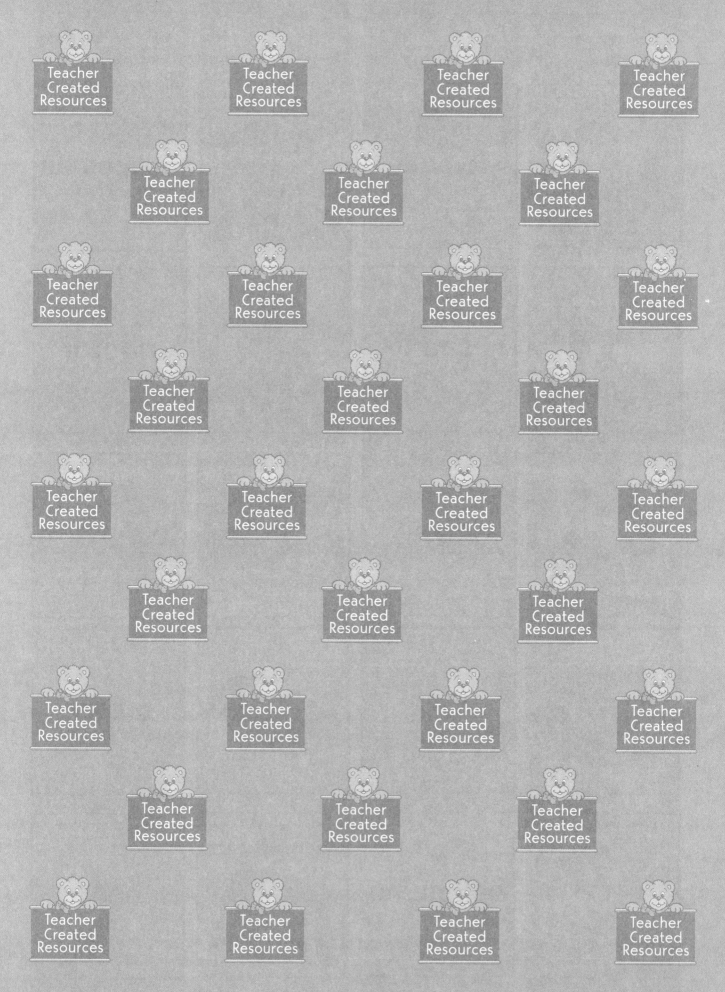

70

	pen		pencil
	crayon		chalk
	computer		book
	newspaper		magazine
	sign		letter

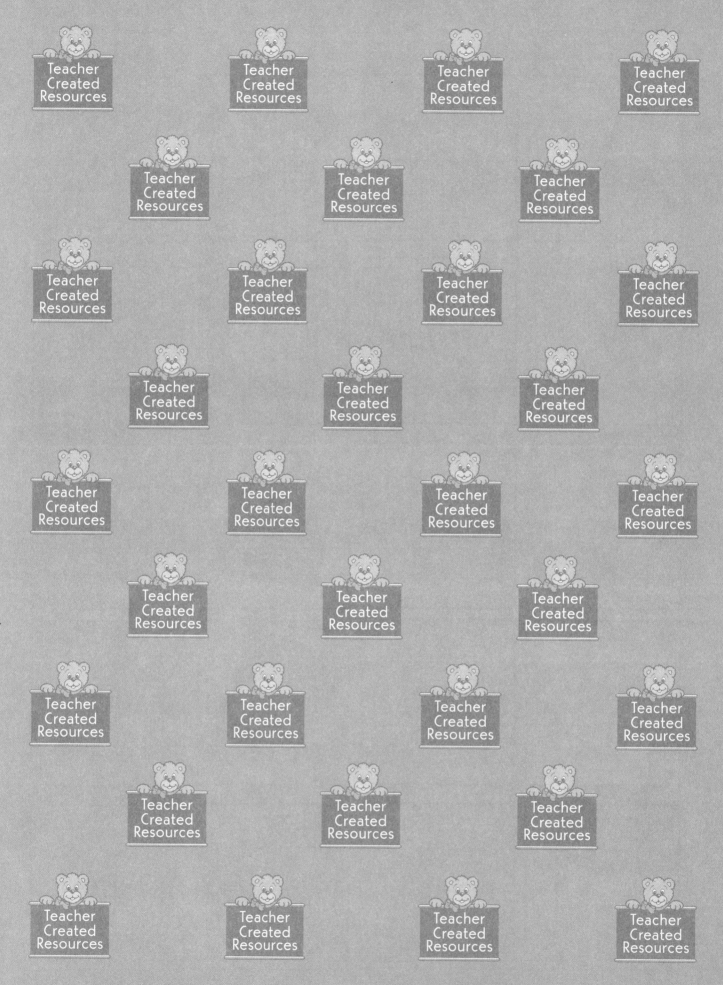

72

678 Numbers 6–10

Fruit

Plants

Sky Things

Earth Things

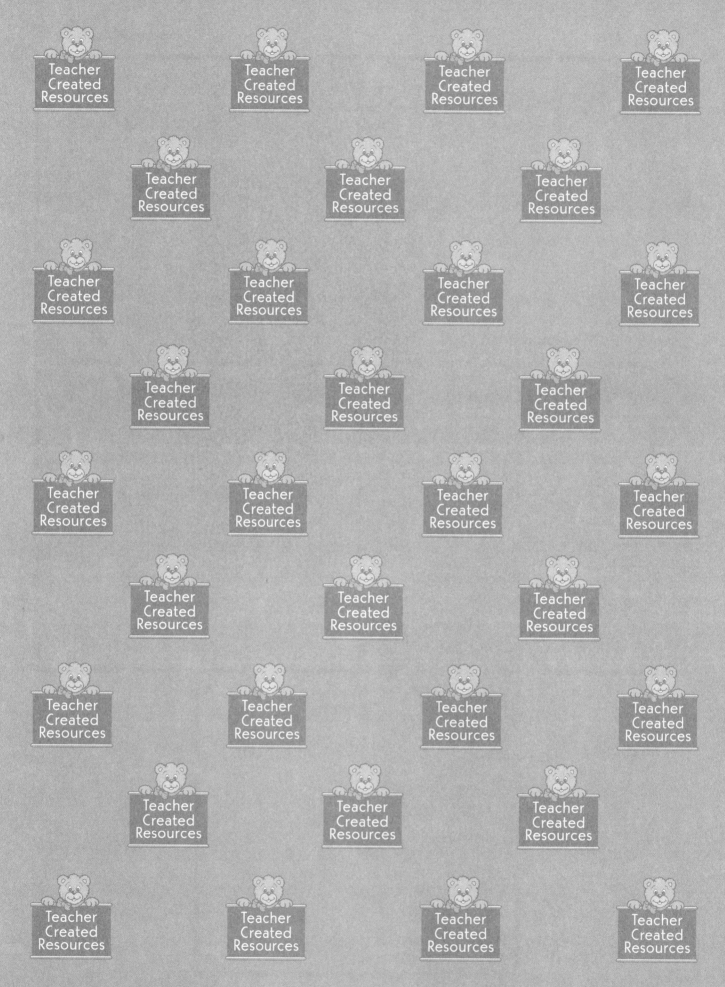

74

Farm Animals

Workers

Entertainment

Writing Tools

Reading Things

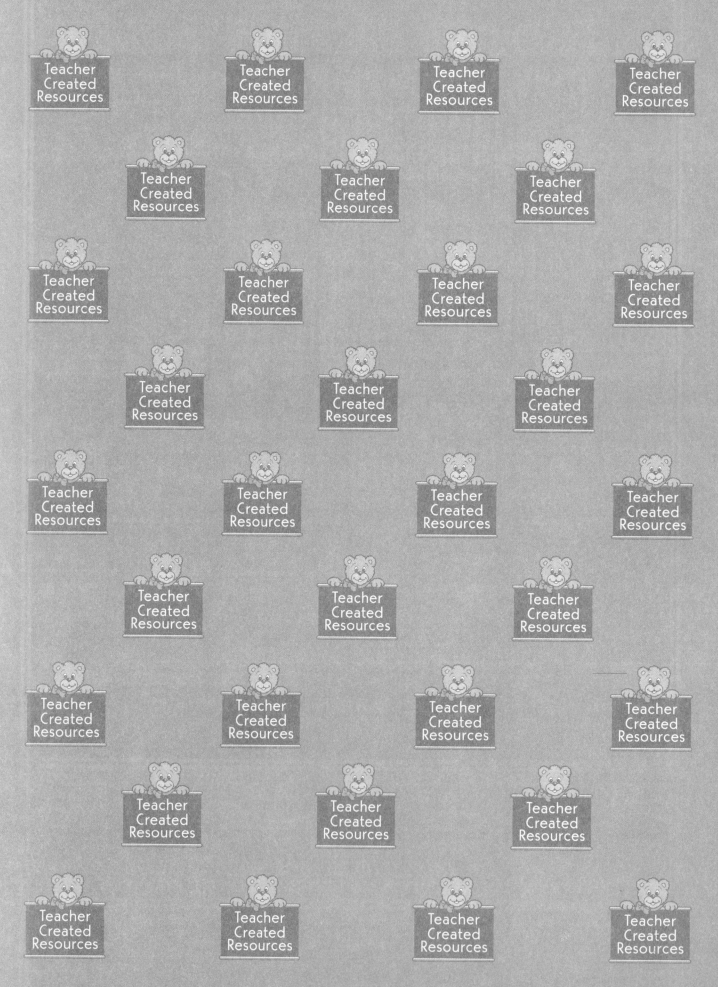

76

Picture Noun P.I.

Skill

- Students find the Picture Noun that fits best in each sentence.

Grouping

- independent
- pairs
- small group

Materials

- Instant Words Sentence Strips (pages 79–95)
- Picture Noun Cards, pictures or words (pages 63–71)
- Picture Noun P.I. Journal (page 78)
- pencils

Directions

1. Write the following sentence on the board:

On the farm there is a ⬚ ? ⬚ .

2. Hold up a few Picture Noun Cards (either words or pictures depending on your students). Make sure one of the cards has a sensible answer.

3. Read the sentence again with the students, filling in the blank with each Picture Noun.

4. Ask students which card makes the most sense.

5. Copy the sentence again, filling in the blank with the Picture Noun word or picture and read the sentence again.

6. Tell students they are going to be Picture Noun private investigators and solve for the missing Picture Nouns in each sentence. Tell students they must look in the sentence for clues to help them find the missing Picture Noun. Once they find a match, they must record their sentences in their journals. (*Note:* Some sentences have more than one correct answer.)

7. Pass out pencils and copies of the Picture Noun P.I. Journal (page 78).

8. Have students choose an Instant Words Sentence Strip. Tell them they must read the sentence first and then choose a card that would make sense.

9. Then, have students read their filled-in sentence to a friend and record it on their papers.

Suggestions

- Laminate the sentence strips and Picture Noun Cards.
- Have students bring in long coats and other detective gear for the day of the activity. Have students use magnifying glasses as they are doing the activity.
- Have students create their own Picture Noun cards that would make sense for the sentences on the strips.

Picture Noun
P.I. Journal

Name: _____ **Date:** _____

Directions: Record your sentences below.

1. _____

_____

2. _____

_____

3. _____

_____

4. _____

_____

5. _____

_____

6. _____

_____

Write a great sentence with your .

Go over the ?. to see a flower.

What is the name of the little ?.

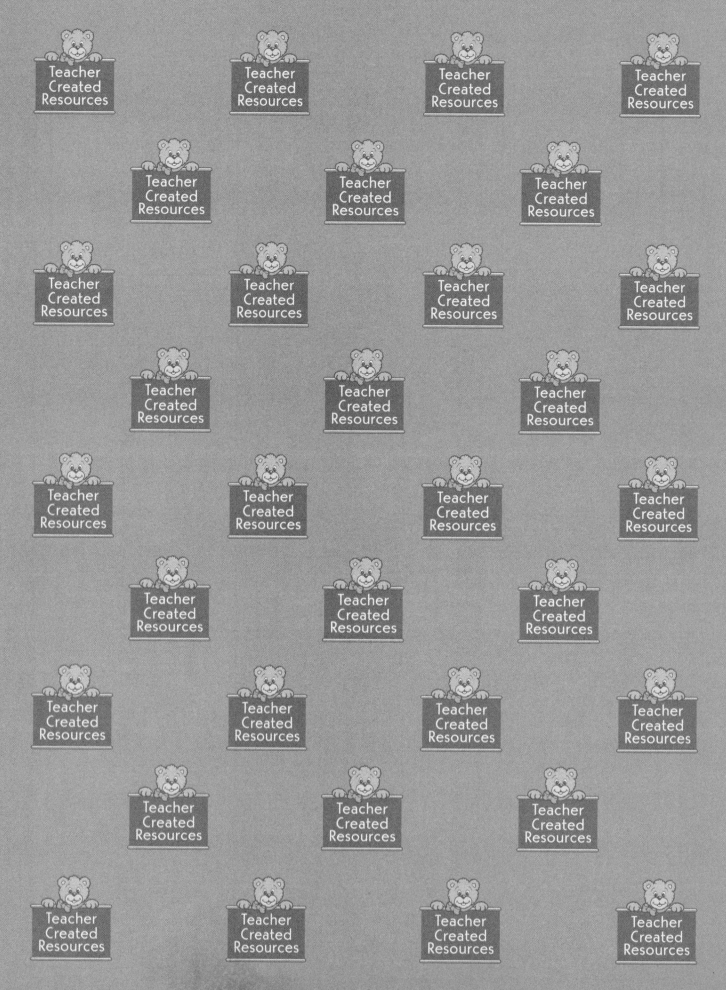

80

These people want to see a

I like an orange more than a

The number before ten is

82

In time, the orange 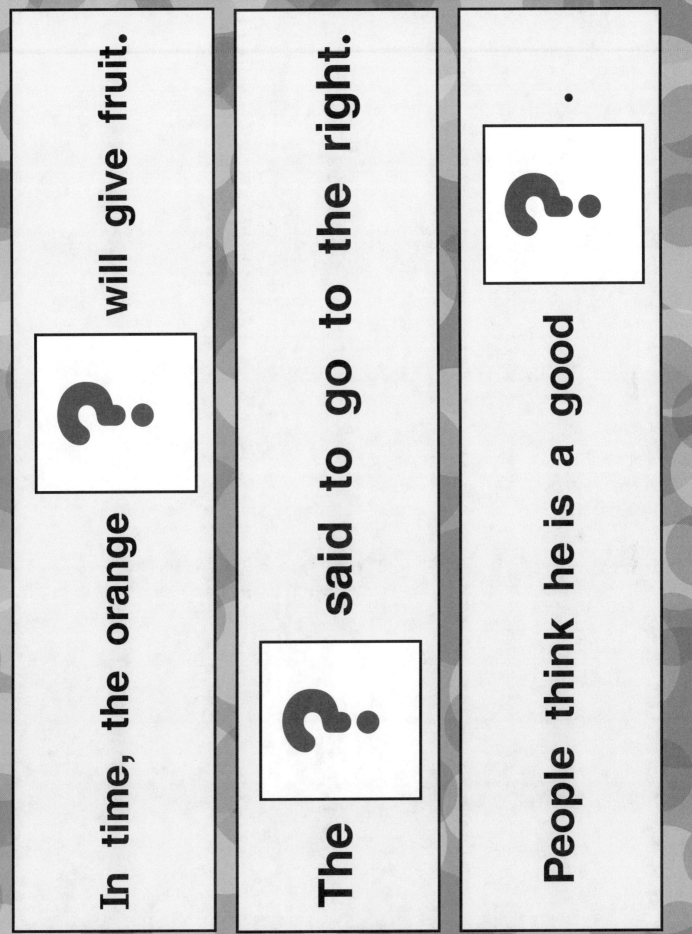 will give fruit.

The 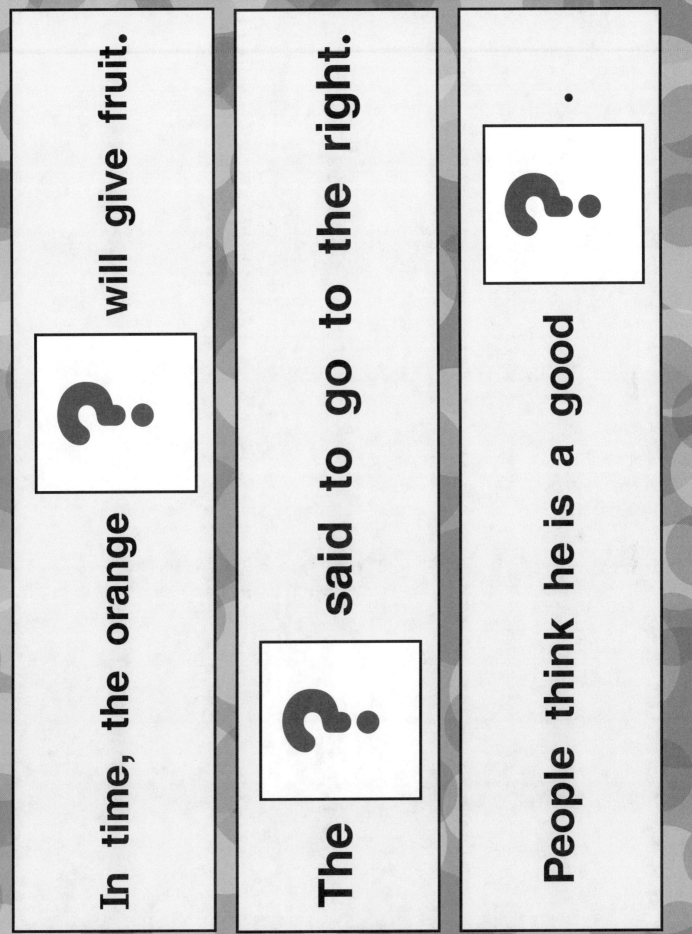 said to go to the right.

People think he is a good 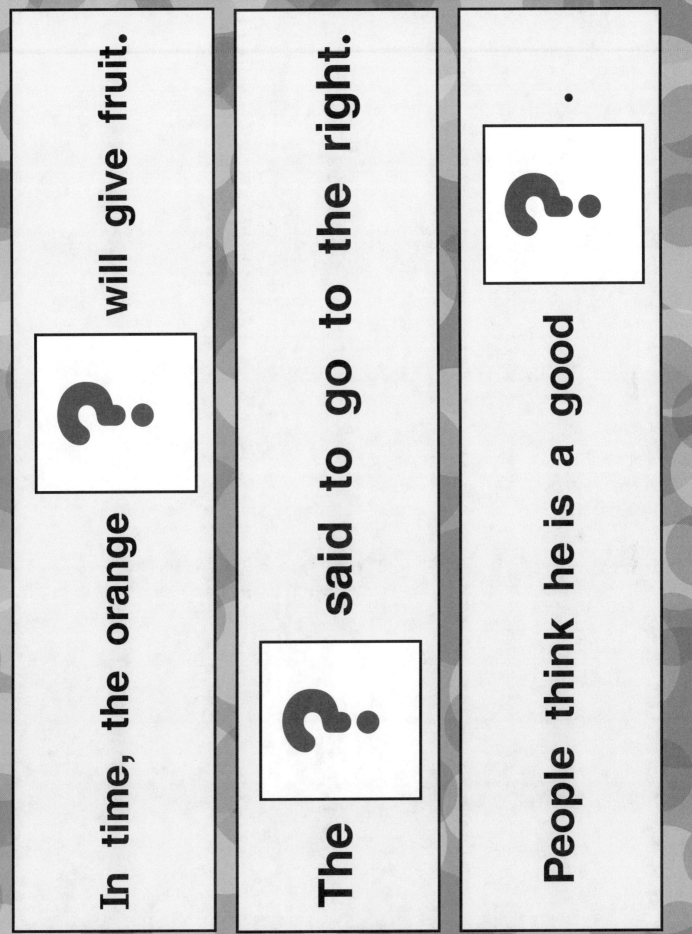 .

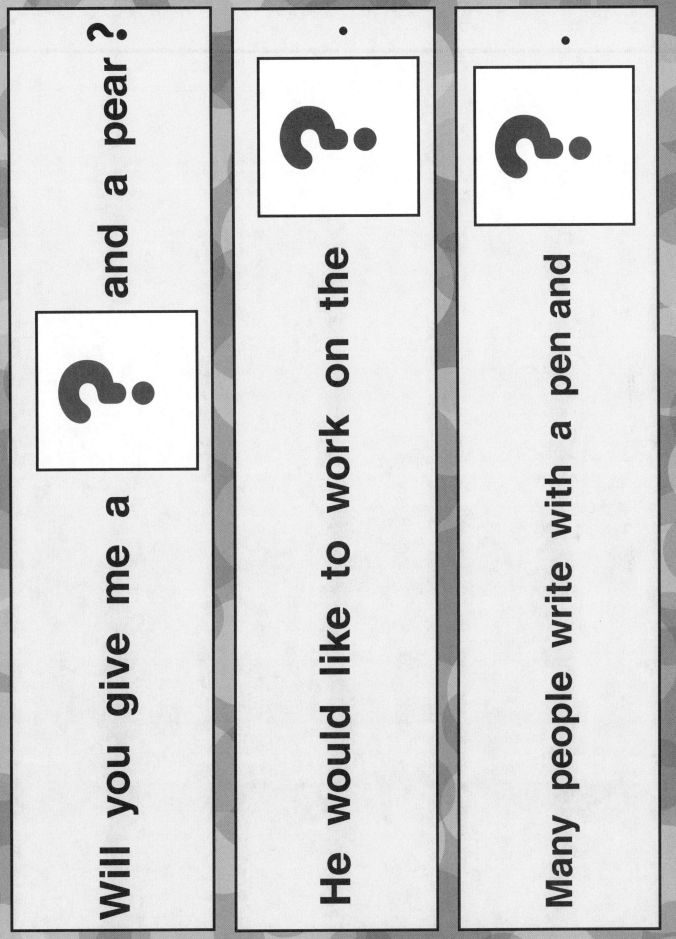

Will you give me a [?] and a pear ?

He would like to work on the [?] .

Many people write with a pen and [?] .

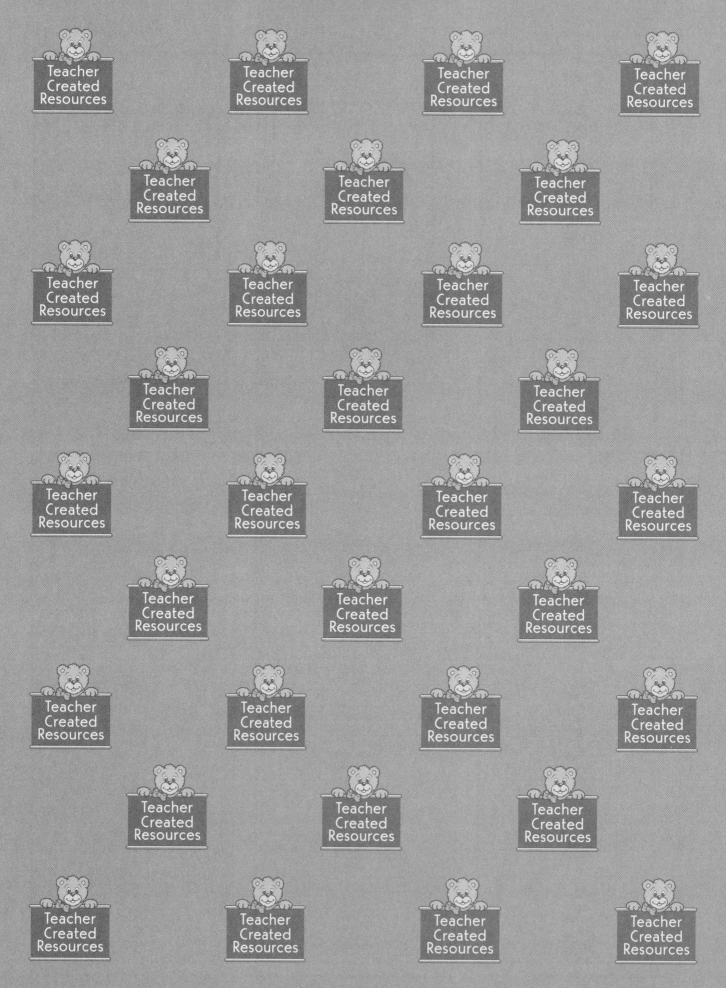

The doctor and [?] will help you.

Look up and see the stars and [?].

Come see the show on the [?].

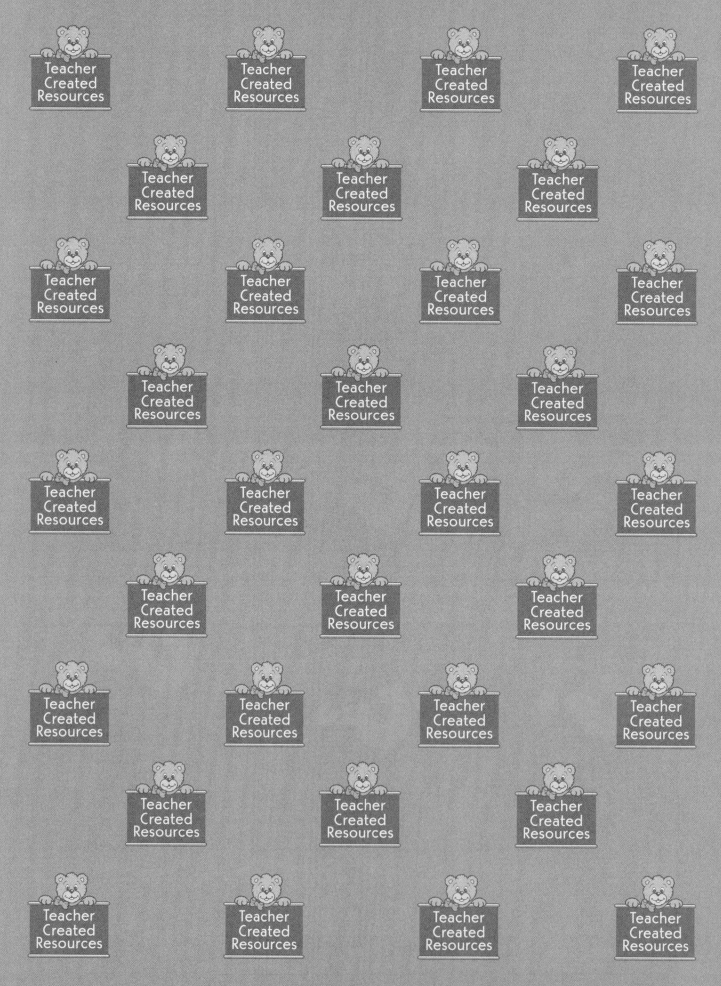

The man has been at his work for  years.

A 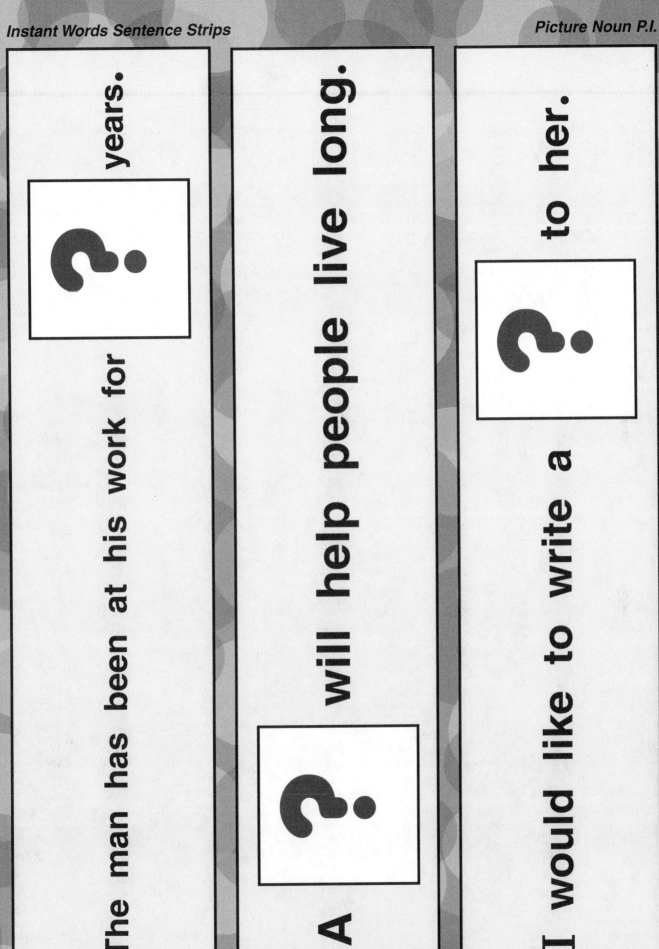 will help people live long.

I would like to write a  to her.

90

The duck and the 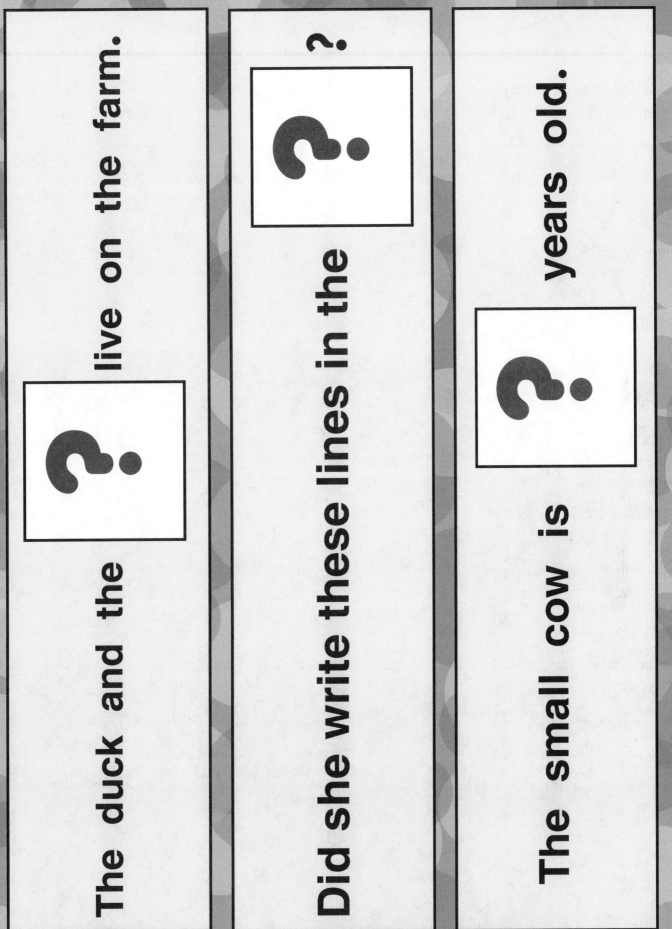 live on the farm.

Did she write these lines in the ?

The small cow is years old.

92

The 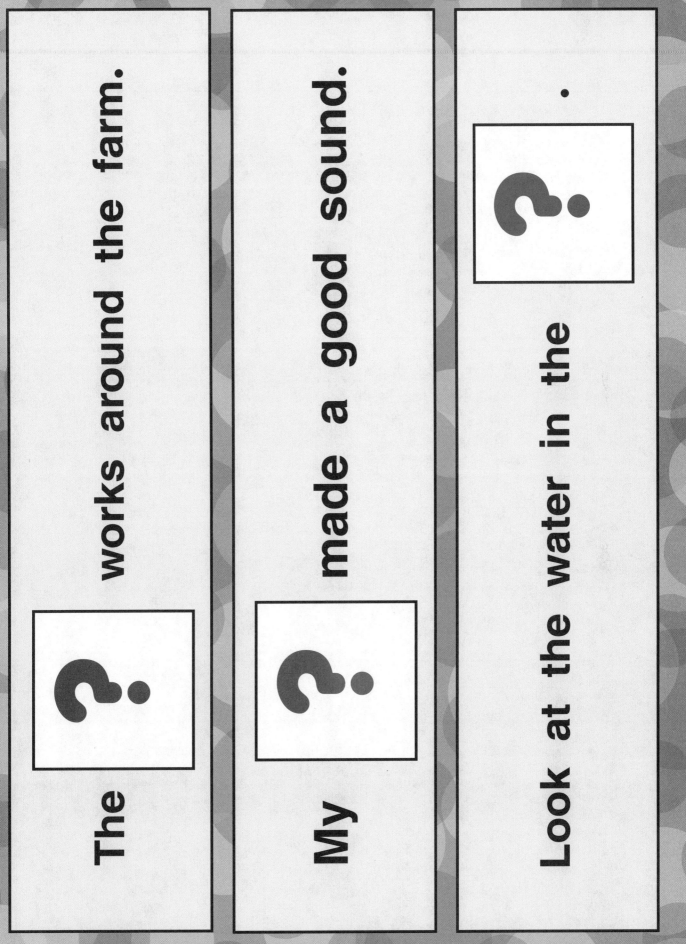 works around the farm.

My made a good sound.

Look at the water in the .

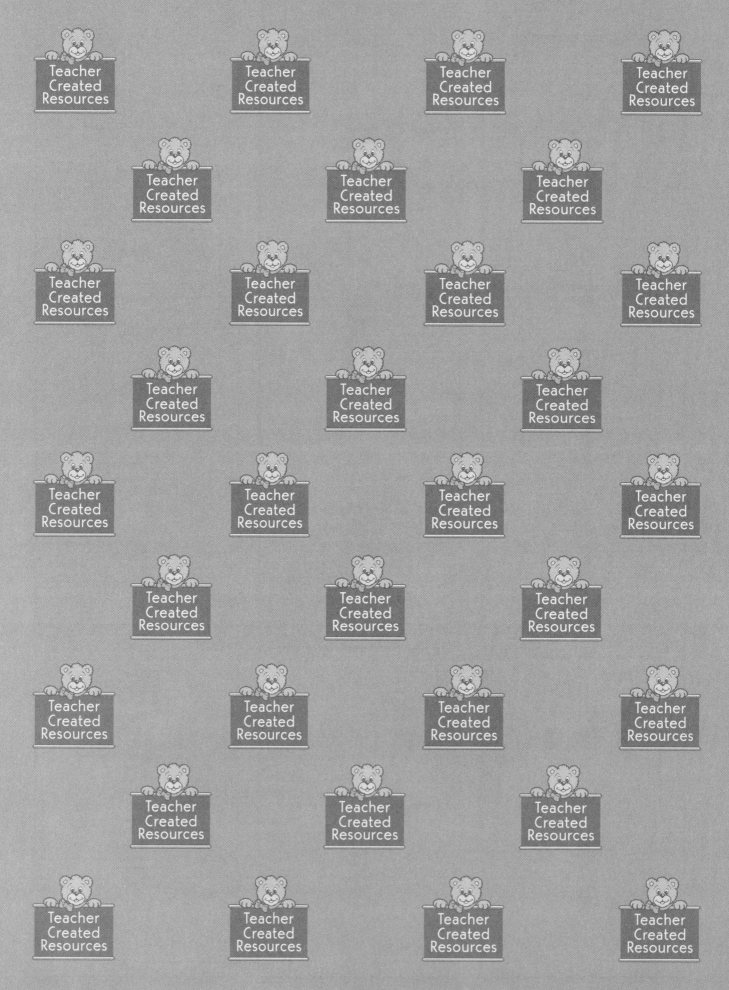

94

The old man called the small 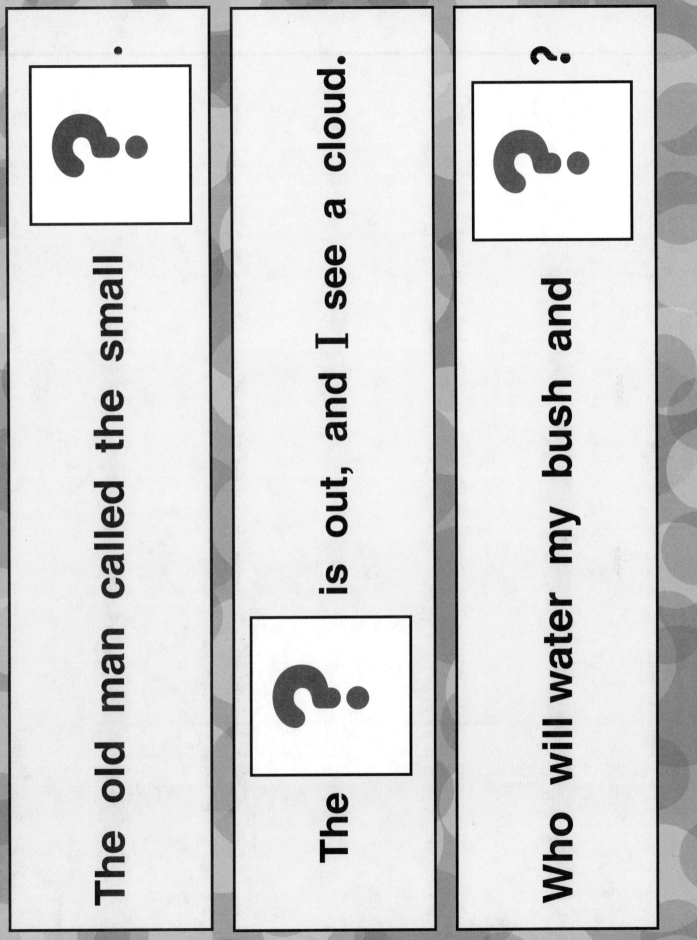.

The 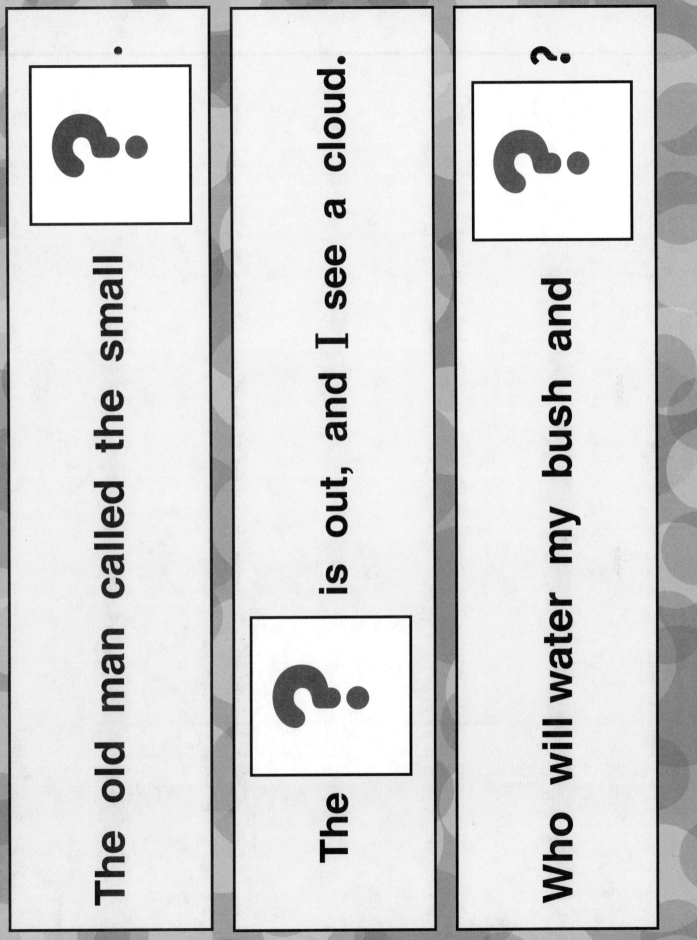 is out, and I see a cloud.

Who will water my bush and 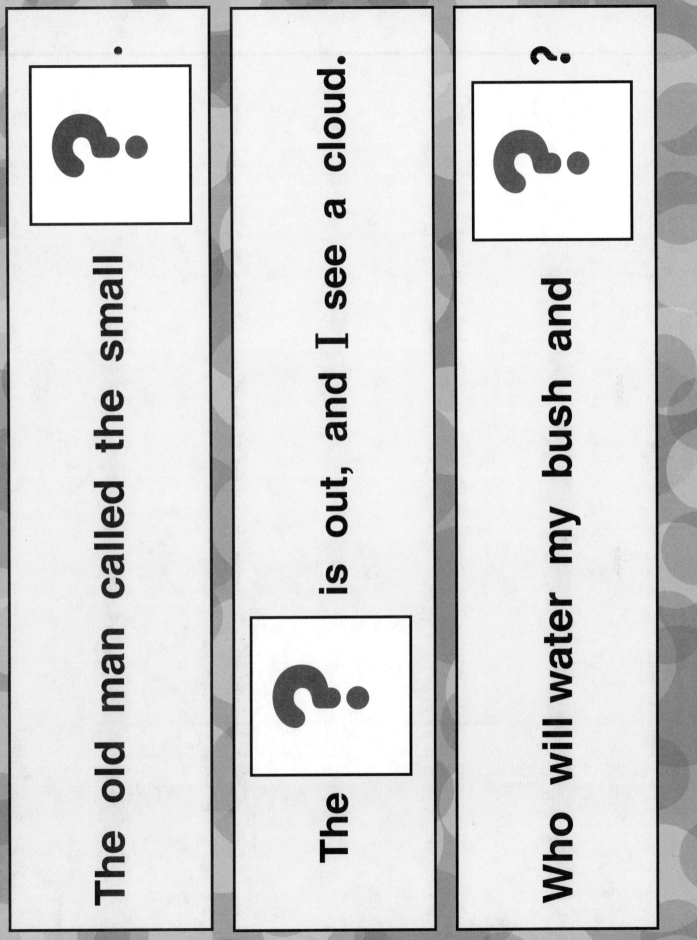?

Sentence Builders

Skill
- Students will use Instant Words 51–150 and Picture Nouns: Sets 11–20 to create and read sentences.

Grouping
- independent
- pairs
- small group

Materials
- Instant Words 51–150 Cards (pages 99–115)
- Picture Noun Cards (pages 63–71)
- Extra Word Cards (page 117)

Directions
1. Place the Picture Nouns (only pictures or pictures and words) and the Instant Words Cards face up on a flat surface.

2. Have students choose cards to create a sentence. A sample is shown below. (*Note:* Extra Instant Words cards are included on page 117 to help put sentences together. Students also can create extra word cards if needed. You can find Instant Words 1–50 Cards in TCR 3148: *Dr. Fry's Reading Activities* (Grades K–1).

3. Have each student read his or her sentence to a friend or to a teacher.
4. Have students create more sentences. Make sure students read each sentence just after they have created it.

Suggestions
- If a student is a beginning reader, then limit the word and picture cards to just a few so that it is not overwhelming for him or her.
- Place a sentence (using the Instant Word Cards and Picture Noun cards) into a plastic bag. Have a student take the cards out and try to create the sentence. Make several bags from which students can choose.
- Make multiple copies of page 98 to reinforce the Instant Words and Picture Nouns. Have students copy their sentences on the worksheet. Remind them to capitalize and punctuate as necessary.
- For a challenge, take the picture cards out. Have students use only the word cards.

Sentence Builders

Name: _____ **Date:**_____

Directions: Record your sentences below.

1. _____

   _____

2. _____

   _____

3. _____

   _____

4. _____

   _____

5. _____

   _____

6. _____

   _____

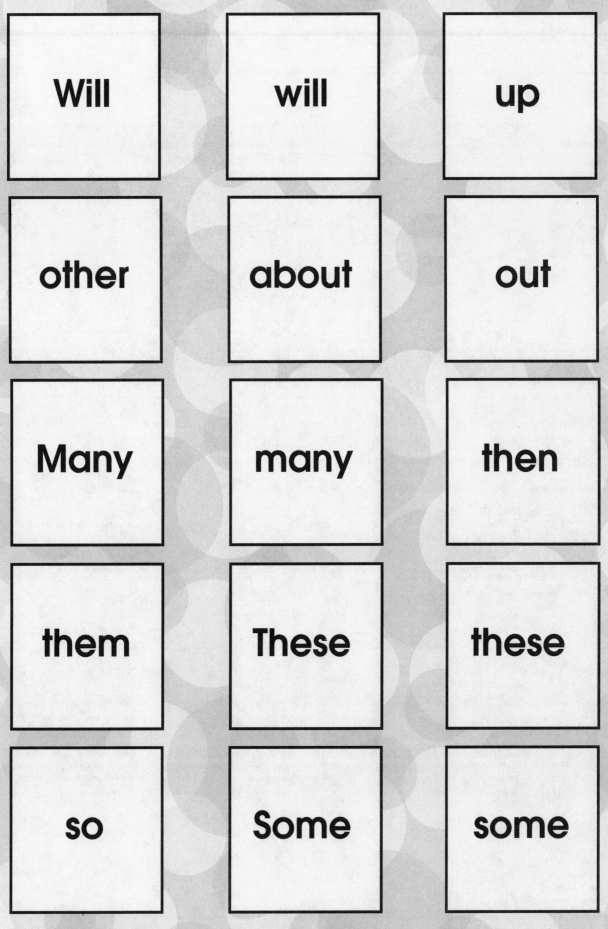

Will	will	up
other	about	out
Many	many	then
them	These	these
so	Some	some

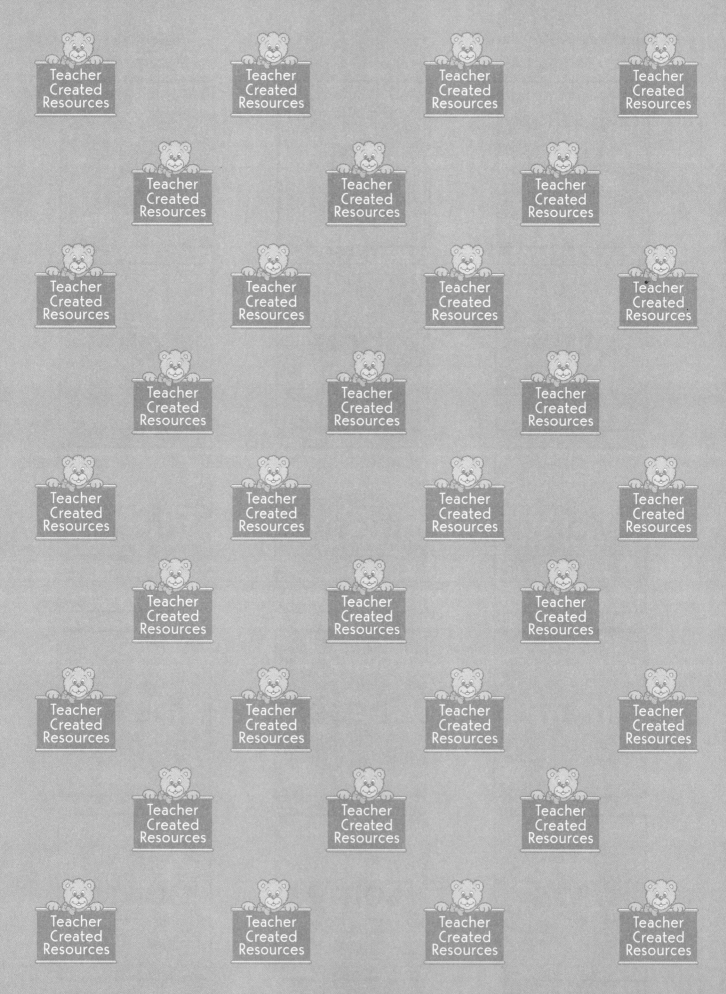

100

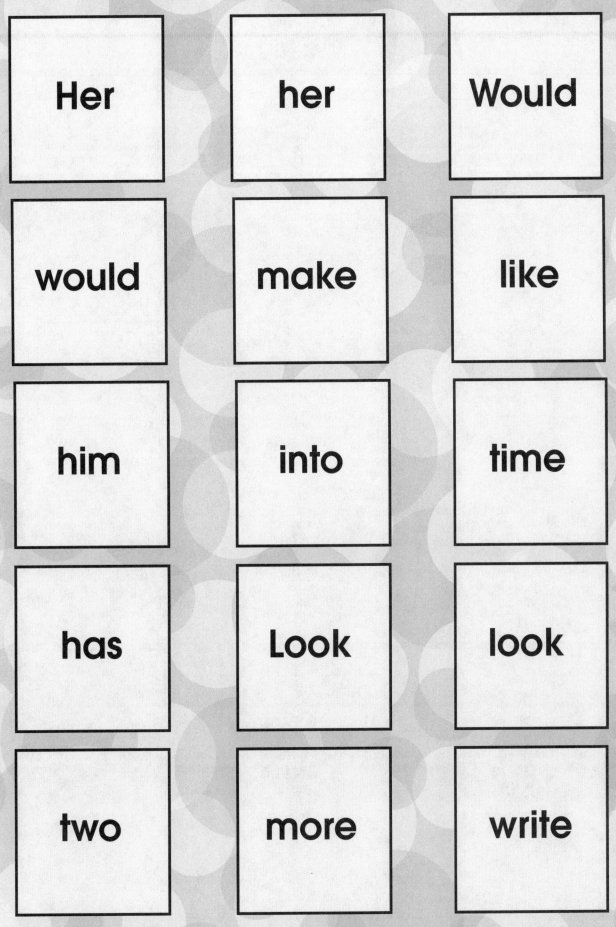

Her	her	Would
would	make	like
him	into	time
has	Look	look
two	more	write

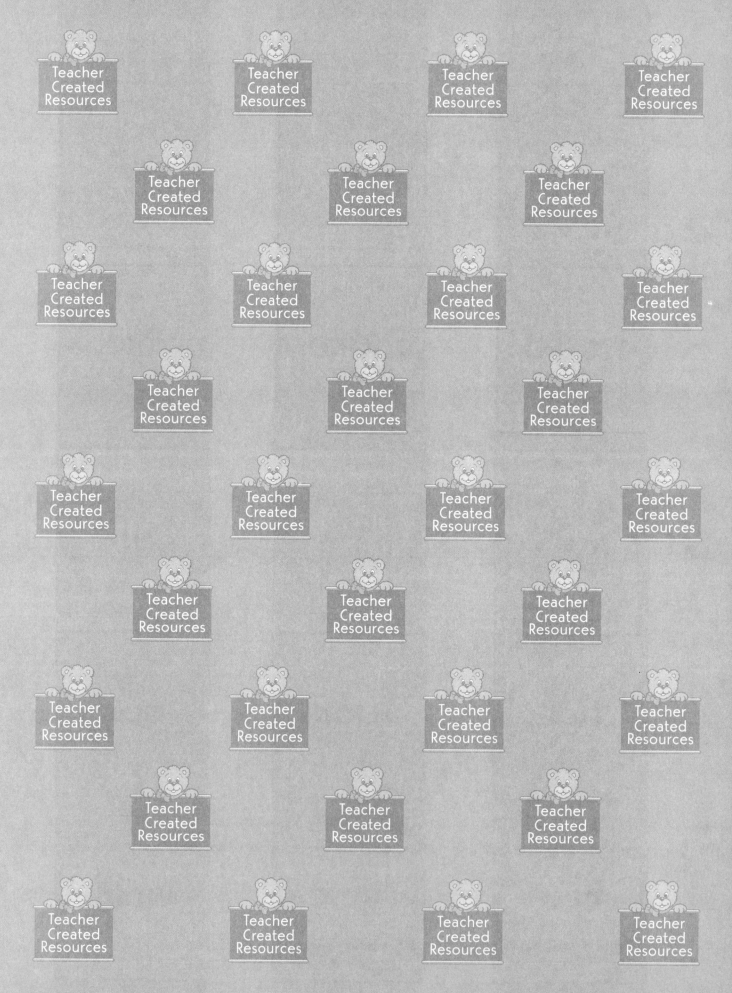

102

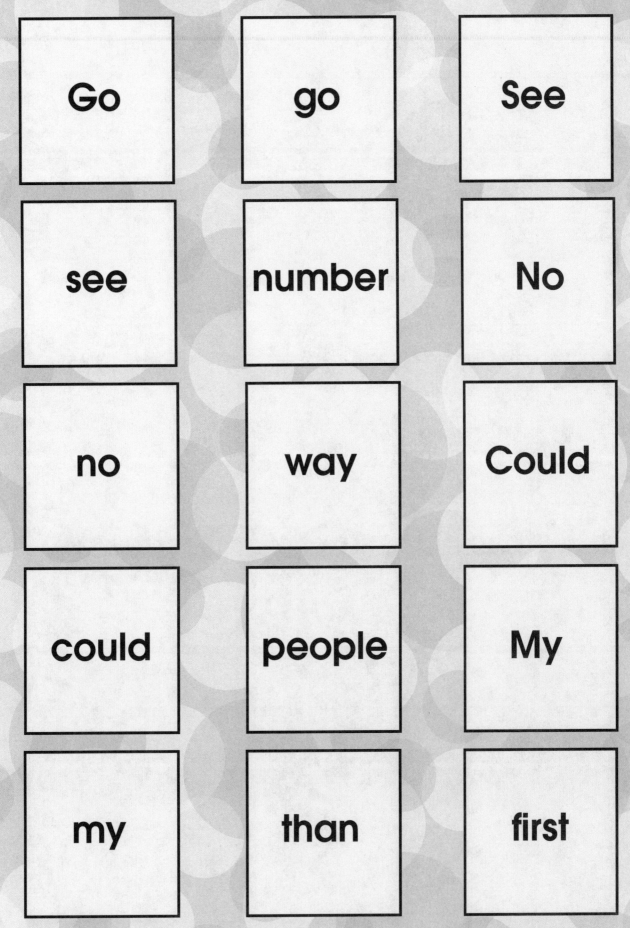

Go	go	See
see	number	No
no	way	Could
could	people	My
my	than	first

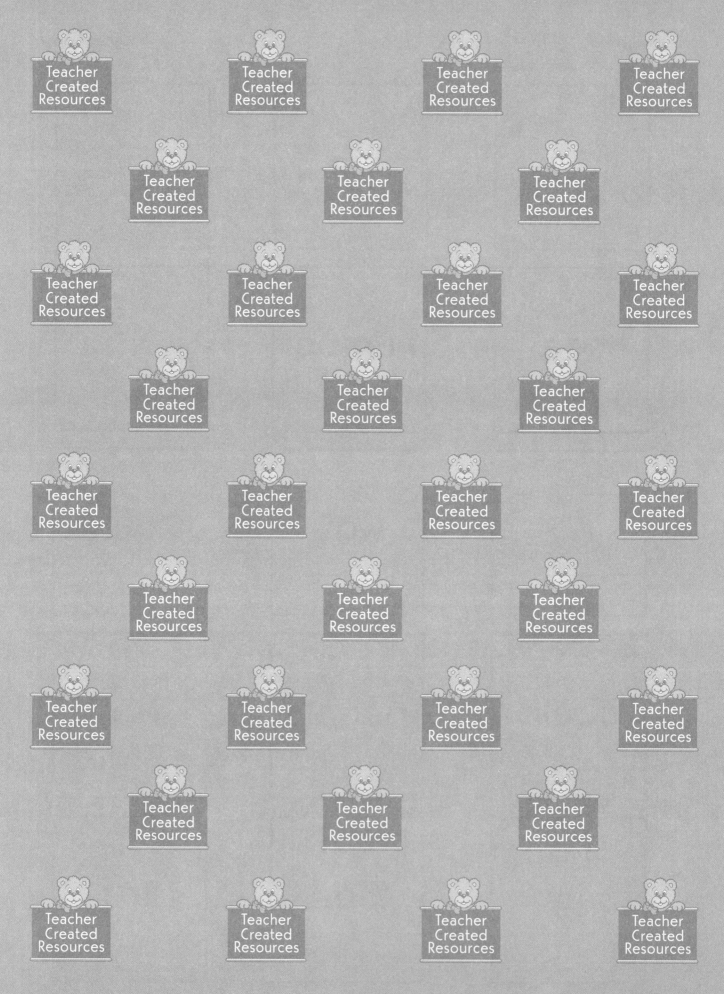

water	been	called
Who	who	am
Its	its	now
Find	find	long
down	day	Did

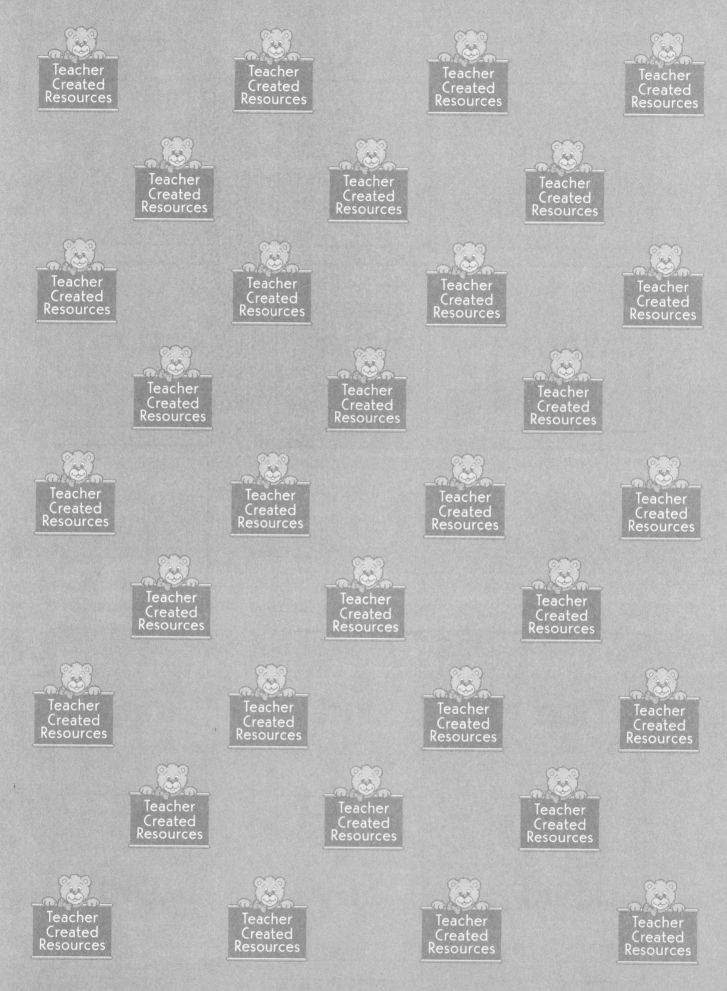

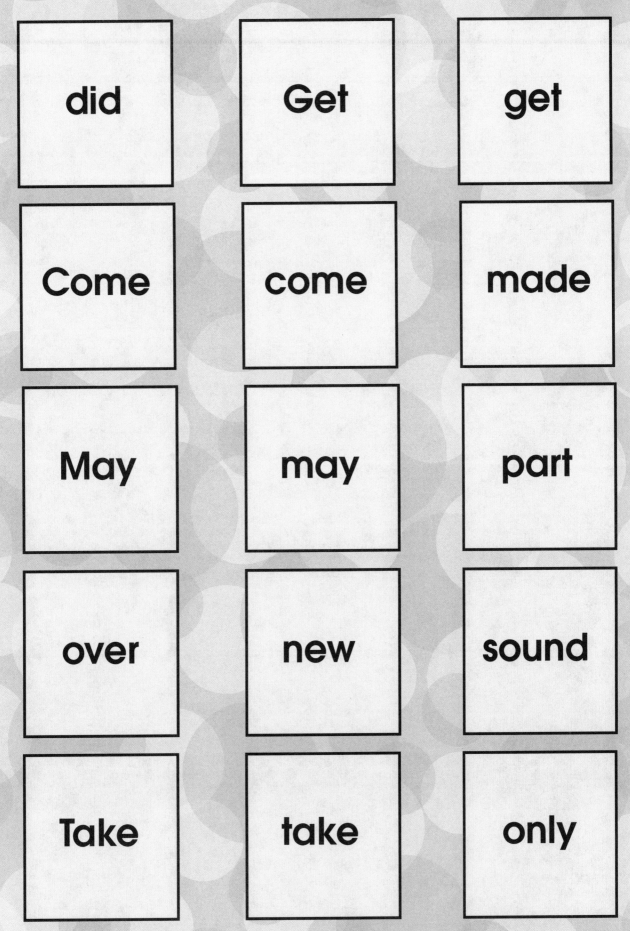

did	Get	get
Come	come	made
May	may	part
over	new	sound
Take	take	only

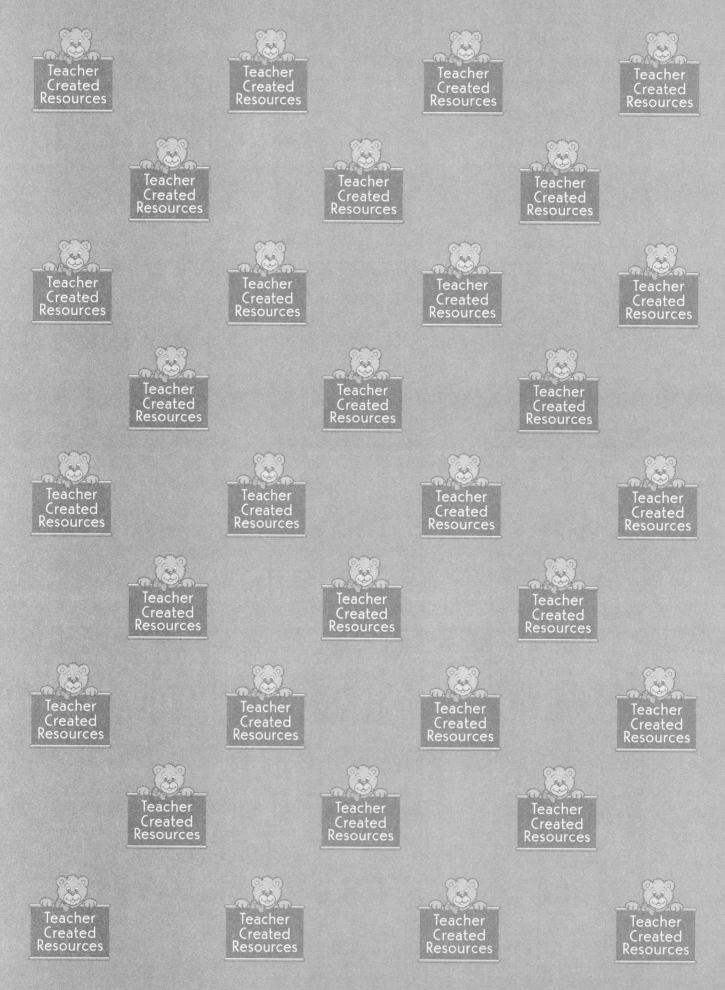

108

little	work	know
place	years	live
me	back	Give
give	Most	most
very	after	things

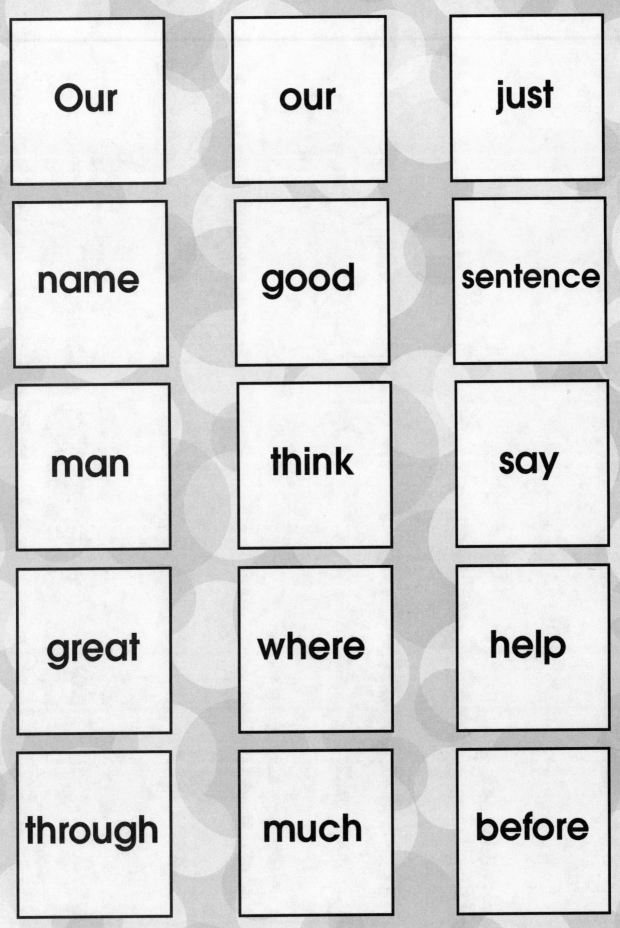

Our	our	just
name	good	sentence
man	think	say
great	where	help
through	much	before

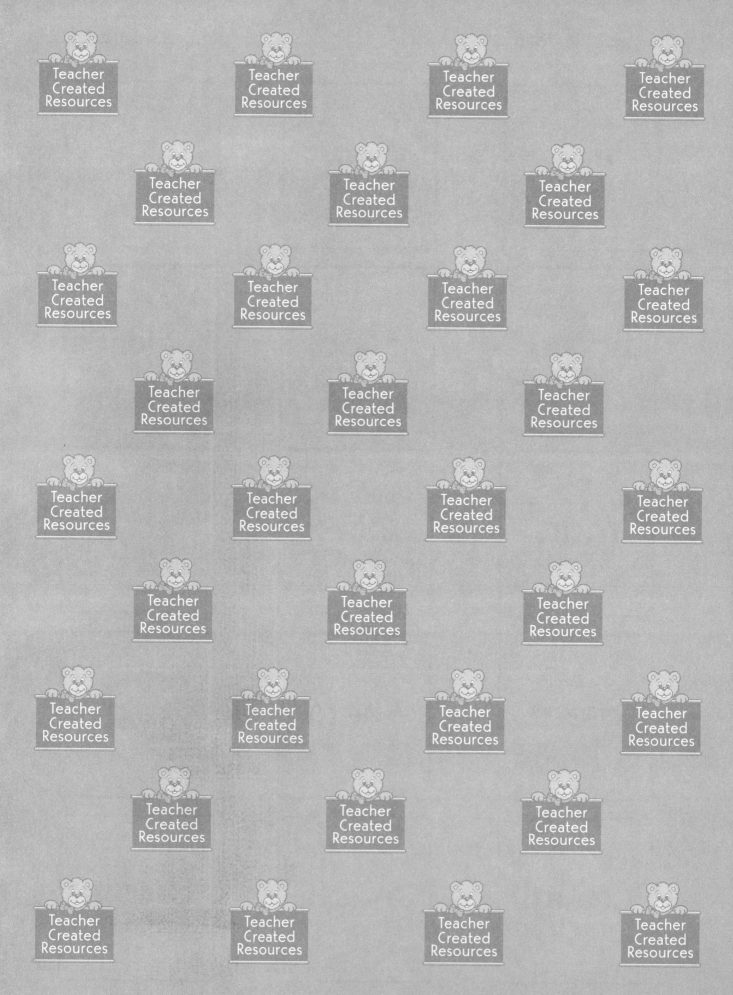

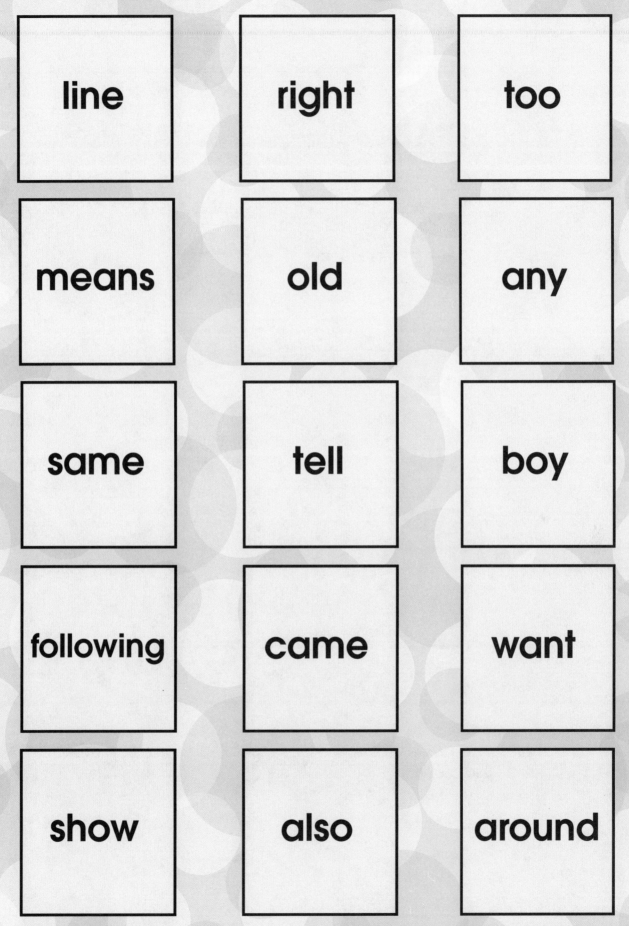

line	right	too
means	old	any
same	tell	boy
following	came	want
show	also	around

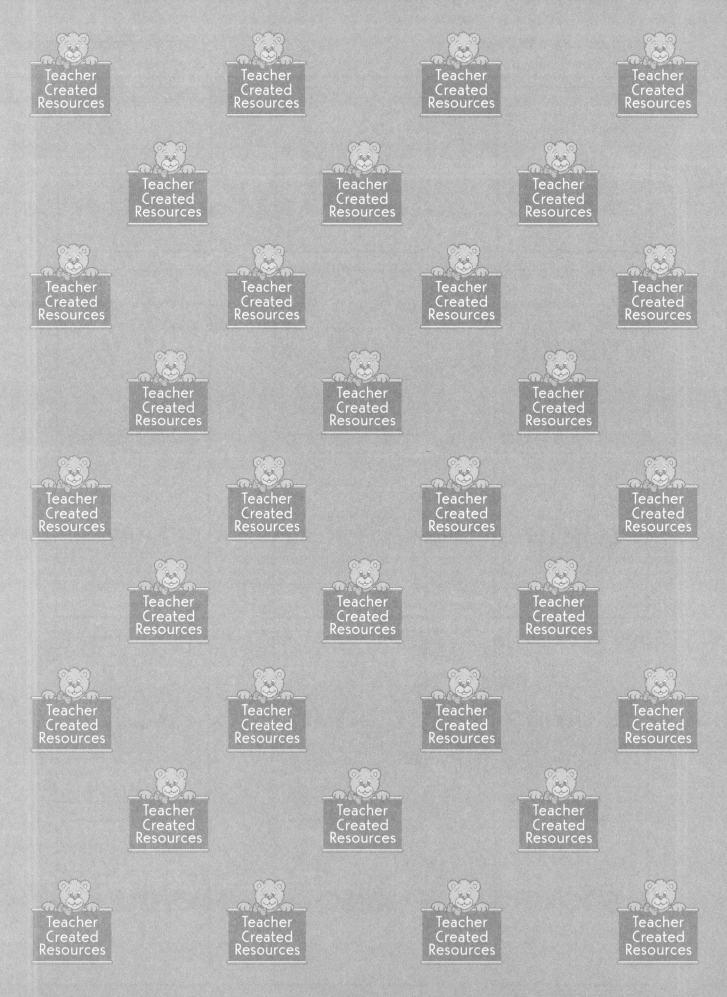

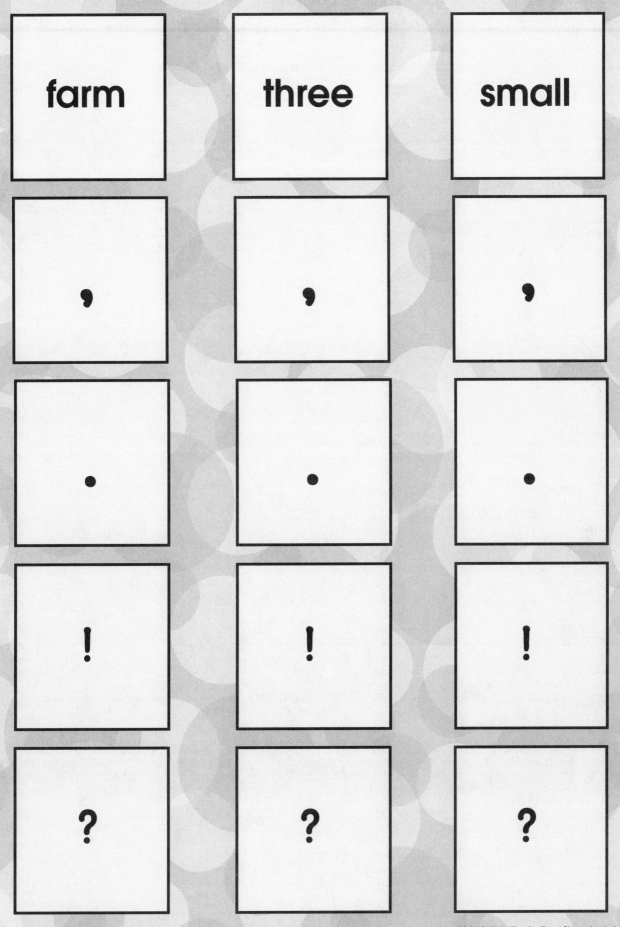

farm	three	small
,	,	,
•	•	•
!	!	!
?	?	?

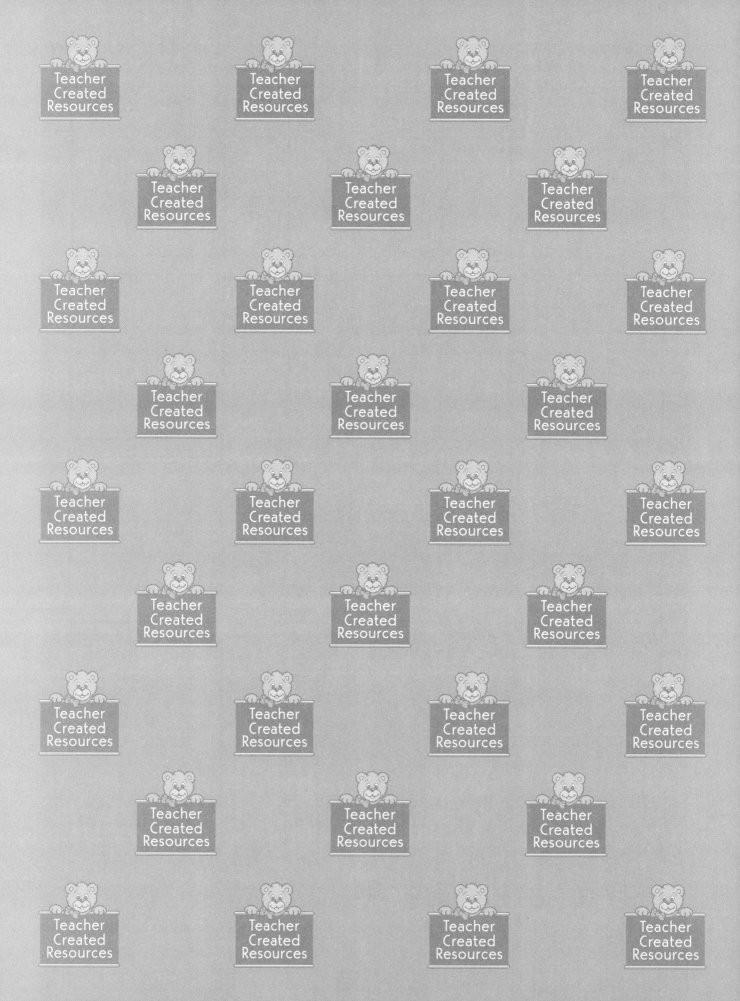

116

A	a	An	an
and	are	at	The
the	Is	is	it
in	on	to	or
but	of	was	with

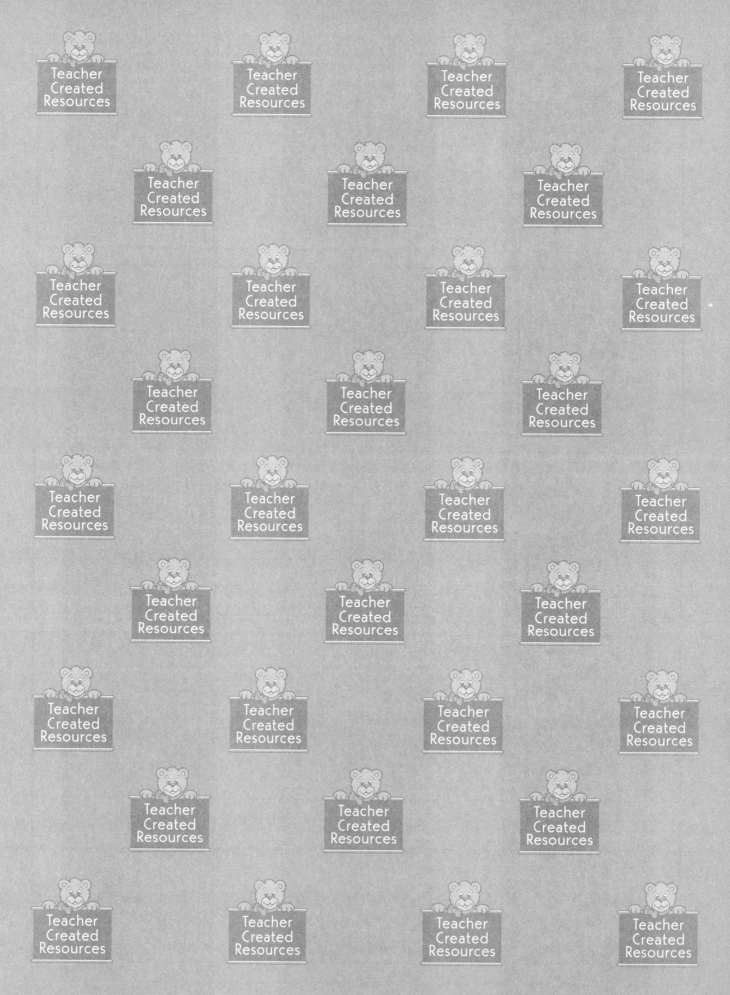

118

Instant Words Activity Boards

Skill
- Students will read Instant Words 51–150.

Grouping
- pairs
- small group
- whole class

Materials
- Instant Words Activity Boards (pages 122–123, 126–127, 130–131, 134–135, or 138–139)
- game marker for each student (coins, colored paper clips, etc.)
- die

Directions
1. Choose one of the following activity boards that suits the needs of your students:

   Instant Words (51–70) Activity Board on pages 122–123

   Instant Words (71–90) Activity Board on pages 126–127

   Instant Words (91–110) Activity Board on pages 130–131

   Instant Words (111–130) Activity Board on pages 134–135

   Instant Words (131–150) Activity Board on pages 138–139

2. Place the activity board on a flat surface with a die.
3. Have students place their markers on the starting area.
4. Have each student take a turn by rolling the die.
5. Have the student move his or her marker the number shown on the die.
6. When the student moves his or her marker, have him or her read the word on the space he or she landed. If the student does not read the word correctly, then the turn is lost. (*Note:* You may leave the option open for the student to ask another student for help.)

Suggestions
- Have students make flashcards of the words they need to learn. Have students take the flashcards home for practice.
- Use the assessment record on page 120 to keep track of which students have successfully read the words on each activity board.
- Have students add the words on the activity board to their personal dictionaries.
- Use the activity boards for centers or send some home with students for individual practice.

Assessment Record

NAME OF STUDENT	Instant Words (51–70) Activity Board	Instant Words (71–90) Activity Board	Instant Words (91–110) Activity Board	Instant Words (111–130) Activity Board	Instant Words (131–150) Activity Board

124

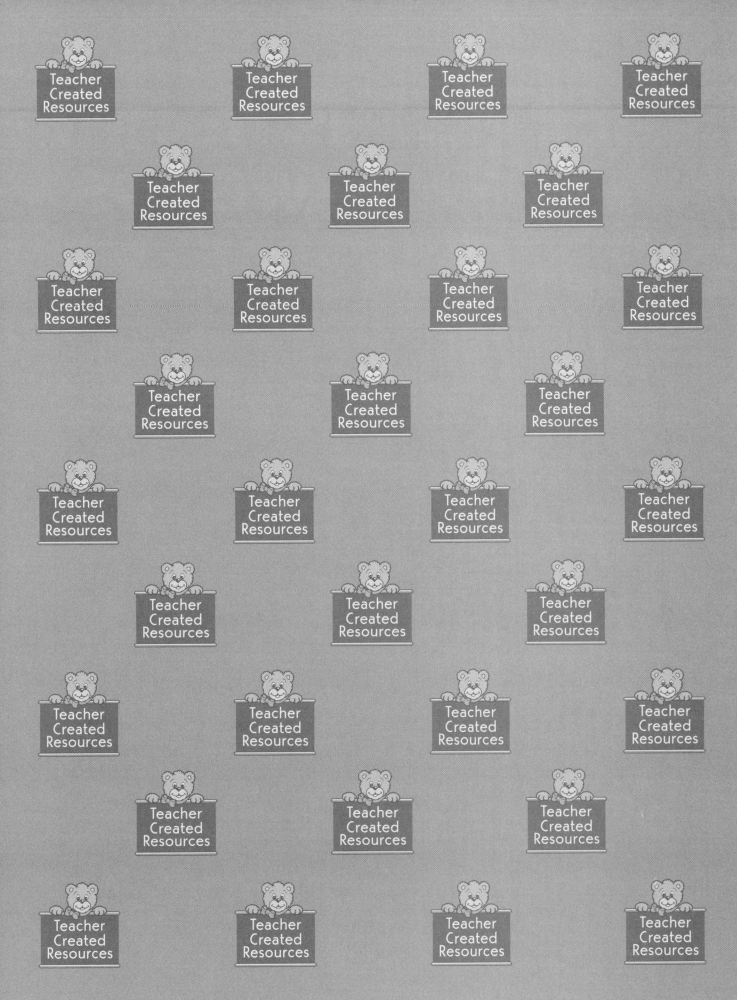

SEA OF INSTANT WORDS

who
am
called
its
been
now
water
than
my
people
could
first
way
FINISH
number
no
see
go
my
more
write
than
two
first
who
called
now
its
am
been
water

128

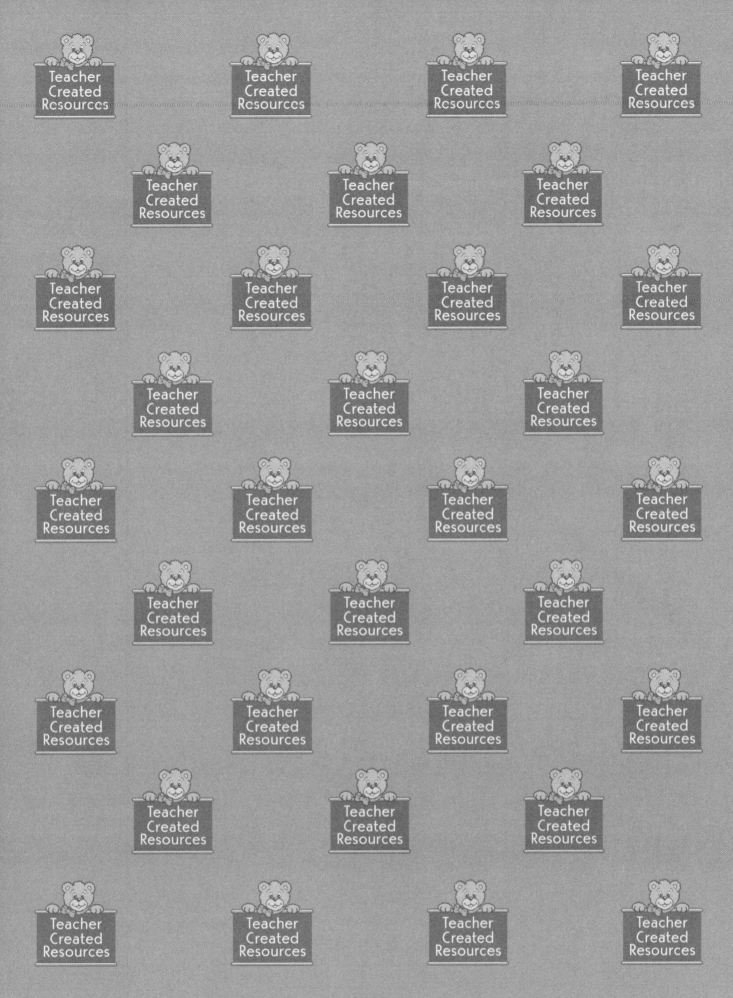

INSTANT WORDS
PET SHOP
ENTRANCE

find
long
down
day
did
get
come
made
may
part
over
new
sound
take
only
little
work
know
place
years
find
long
down
day
did
get
come
made
may
part

EXIT

over
new
sound
take
only
little
work
know
place
years
find
long
down
day
did
get
come
made
may
part
over
new
sound
take
only
little
work
know
place
years

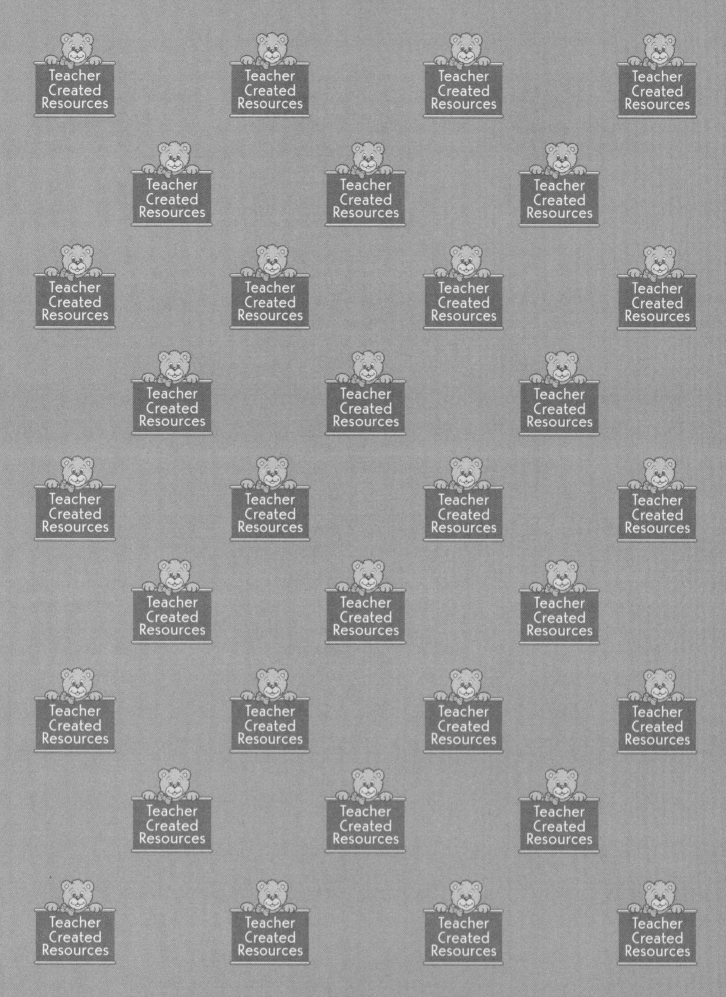

132

A Garden Instant

Full of Words

Finish

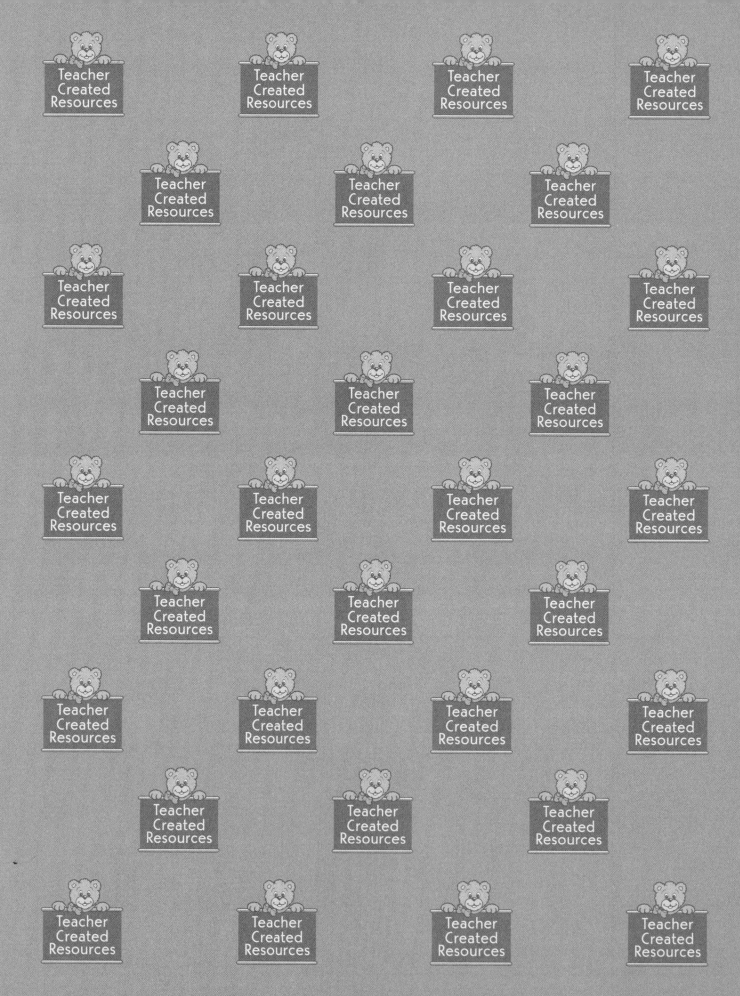

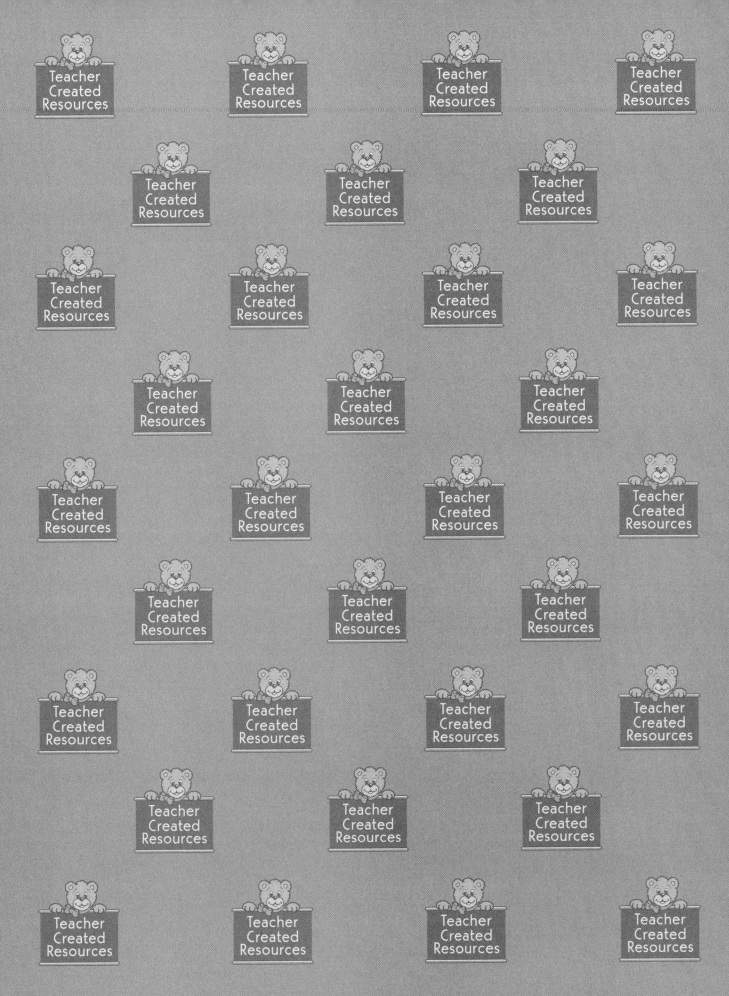

#3149 Dr. Fry's Reading Activities

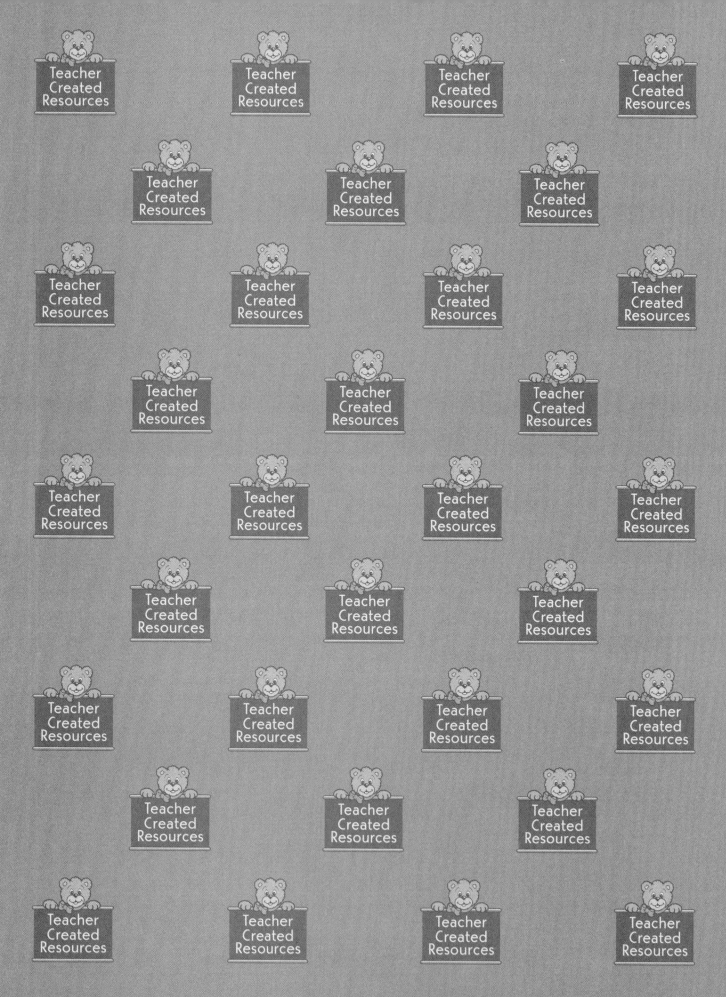

Perfect Pairs

Skill
- Students will learn Instant Words 51–150.

Grouping
- two to five people

Materials
- one of the following four decks of Perfect Pairs cards (Fifty cards are in each deck.)

  Instant Words 51–75 Deck (pages 143–149)   Instant Words 101–125 Deck (pages 155–161)

  Instant Words 76–100 Deck (pages 149–155)   Instant Words 126–150 Deck (pages 161–167)

Directions
1. Pick one of the four decks. Have a student deal five cards to each player.
2. Place the remainder of the deck in the center of the table face down.
3. Tell students that the object of the game is to get as many pairs as possible. Tell them that there are only two cards alike in each deck.
4. The player to the right of the dealer may ask any other player for a specific card. For example, "Do you have *will*?" The player asking must have the mate (in the example, the *will* card) in his or her hand.
5. The player who is asked must give up the card if he or she has it. If the first player does not get the card asked for, then he or she draws one card from the pile.
6. The next player has a turn asking for a card.
7. If the player succeeds in getting the card asked for either from another player or from the pile, then he or she gets another turn. If the player gets a pair, then it is placed down in front of him or her. The player with the most pairs at the end of the game wins. If the player doing the asking does not know how to read the word on the card, then he or she may ask any of the other players or anyone present. If the player who is asked for a card does not know how to read that word, the best thing to do is ask to see the card of the other player requesting the card or ask a non-playing person who can read to look at it. (*Note:* Extra blank cards are provided on page 167 to make color copies for adding more words.)

Suggestions
- Match the decks to the level of the students. Students should know some but not all of the words used in a particular deck. They should have help in playing until they know almost all the words and can get along by themselves. They should play the game on several occasions until they can call out all the words instantly. For beginning readers, use only the easier words to create a custom deck.
- Have students record their pairs on the recording sheet on page 142.
- Lay the cards face down on a flat surface. Play a game of Memory. Each player turns over two cards. If they are a pair, then he or she keeps them. If they are not a pair, then the cards must be put back in exactly the same place, face down. Students must remember the location of cards so one can make a pair with each two cards turned up. The students must read aloud each card turned over. If he or she doesn't know how to read the card, then another player can read the word aloud.

Perfect Pairs Recording Sheet

Name: _____ Date: _____

Directions: Record your word pairs below.

Word Pair 1: _____ _____

Word Pair 2: _____ _____

Word Pair 3: _____ _____

Word Pair 4: _____ _____

Word Pair 5: _____ _____

Word Pair 6: _____ _____

Word Pair 7: _____ _____

Word Pair 8: _____ _____

Word Pair 9: _____ _____

Word Pair 10: _____ _____

Word Pair 11: _____ _____

Word Pair 12: _____ _____

Word Pair 13: _____ _____

Word Pair 14: _____ _____

Word Pair 15: _____ _____

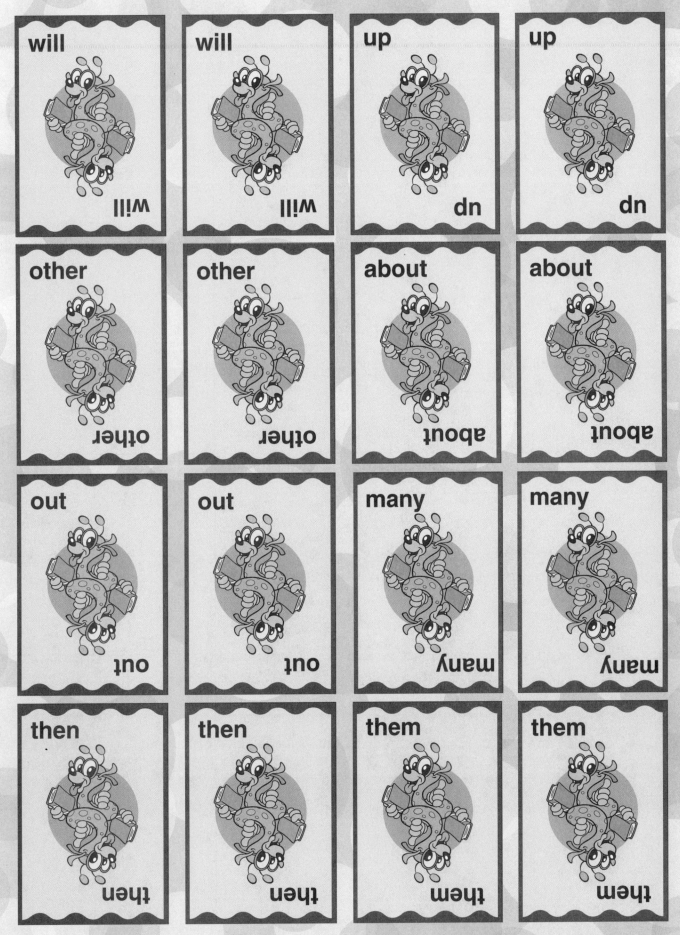

144

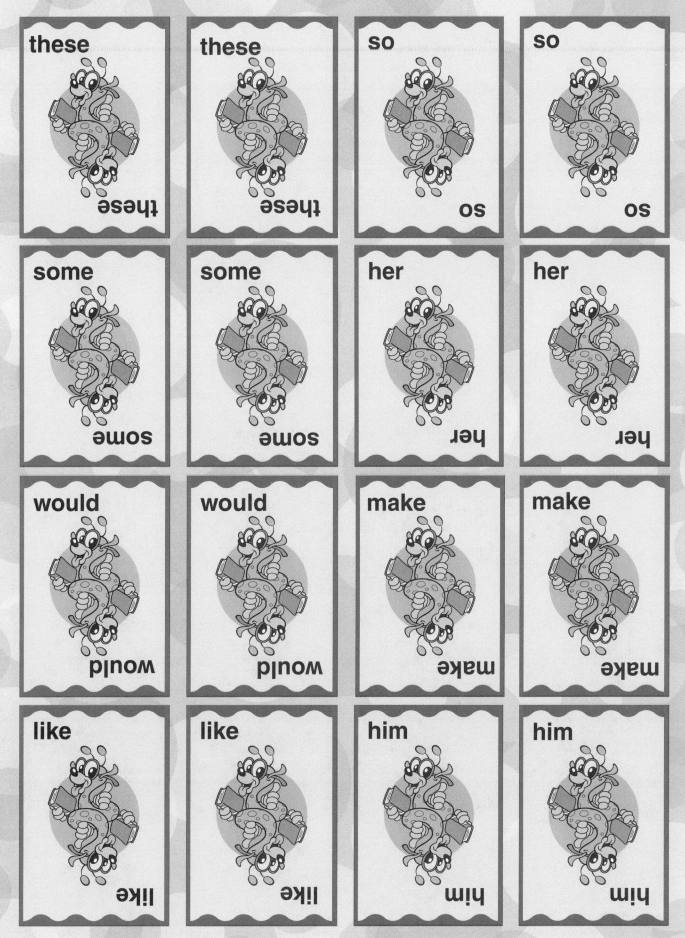

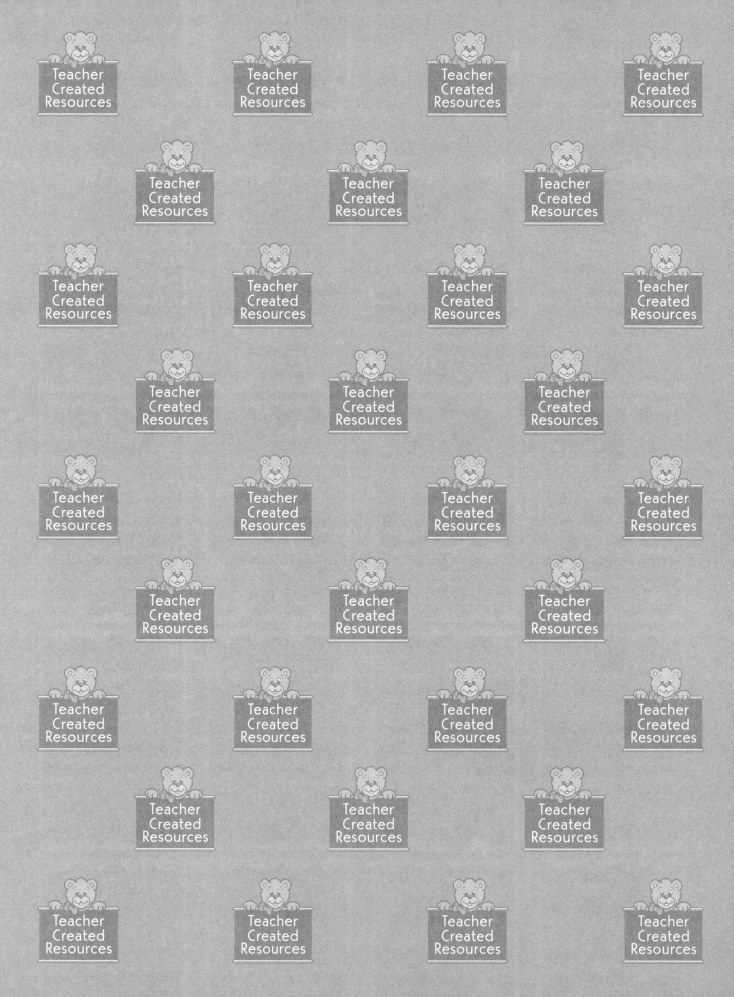

146

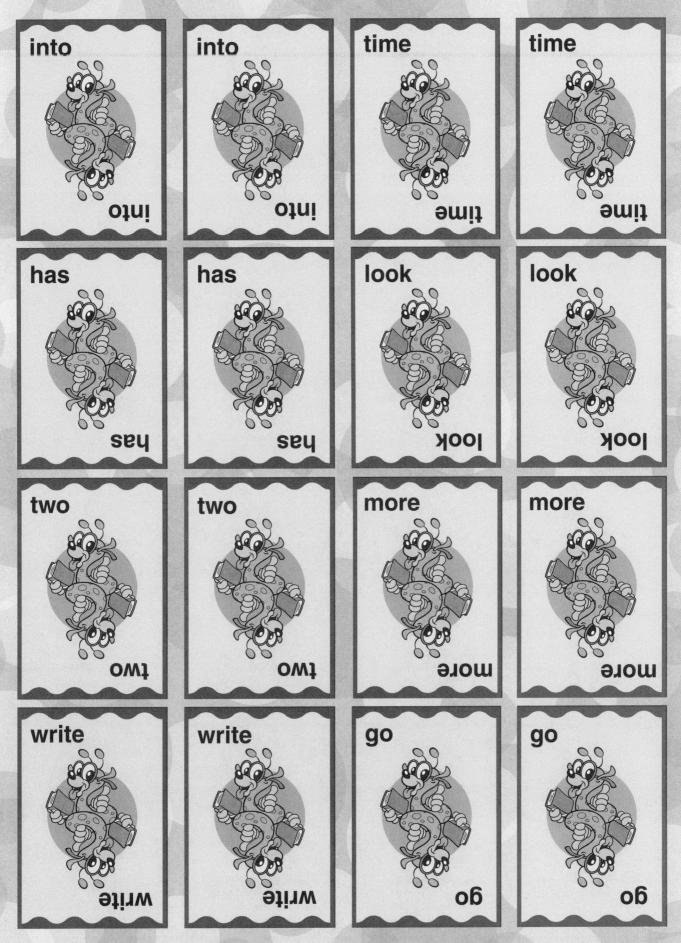

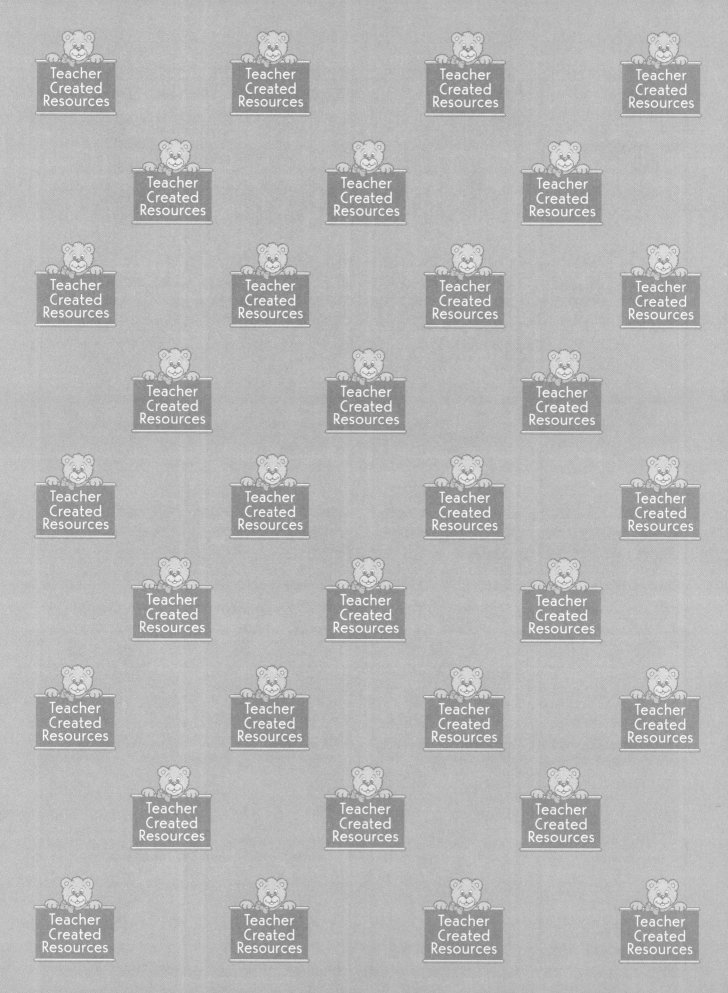

148

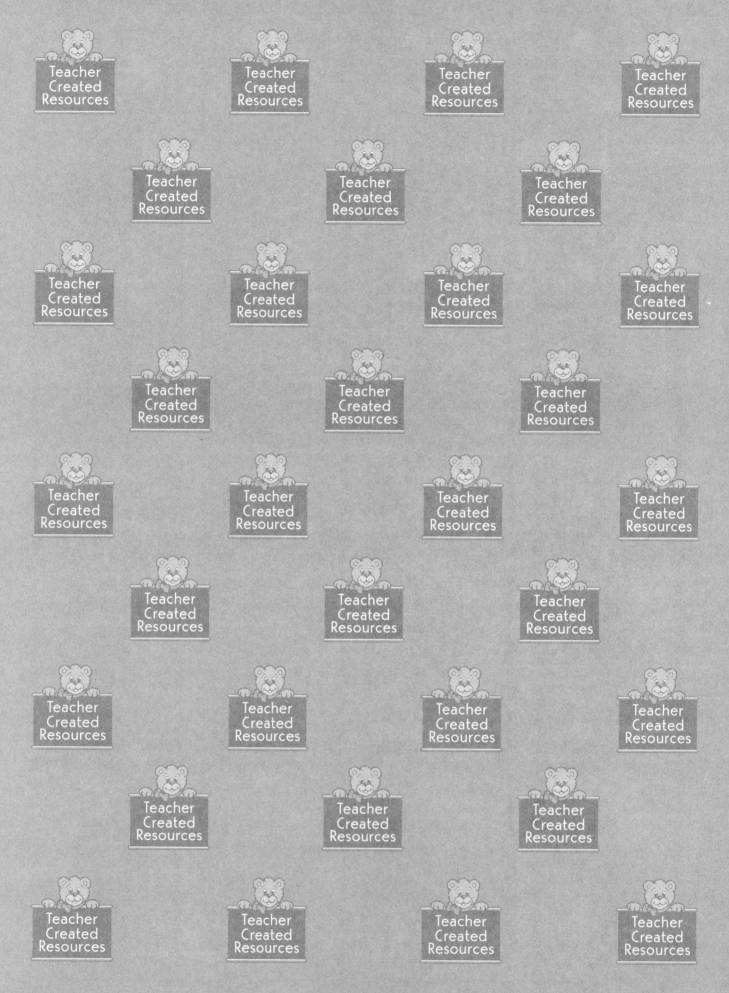

150

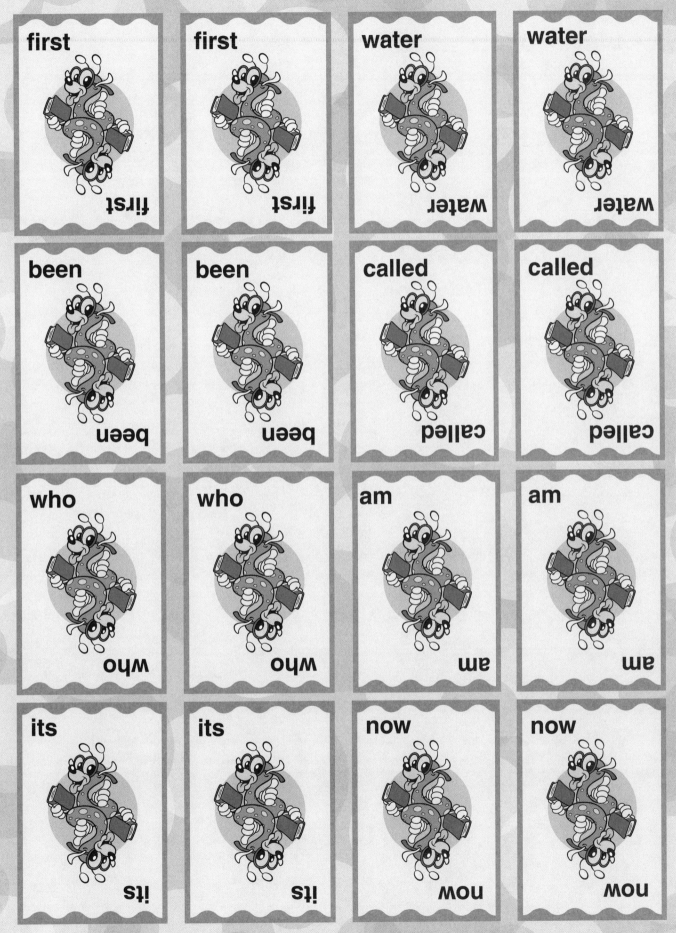

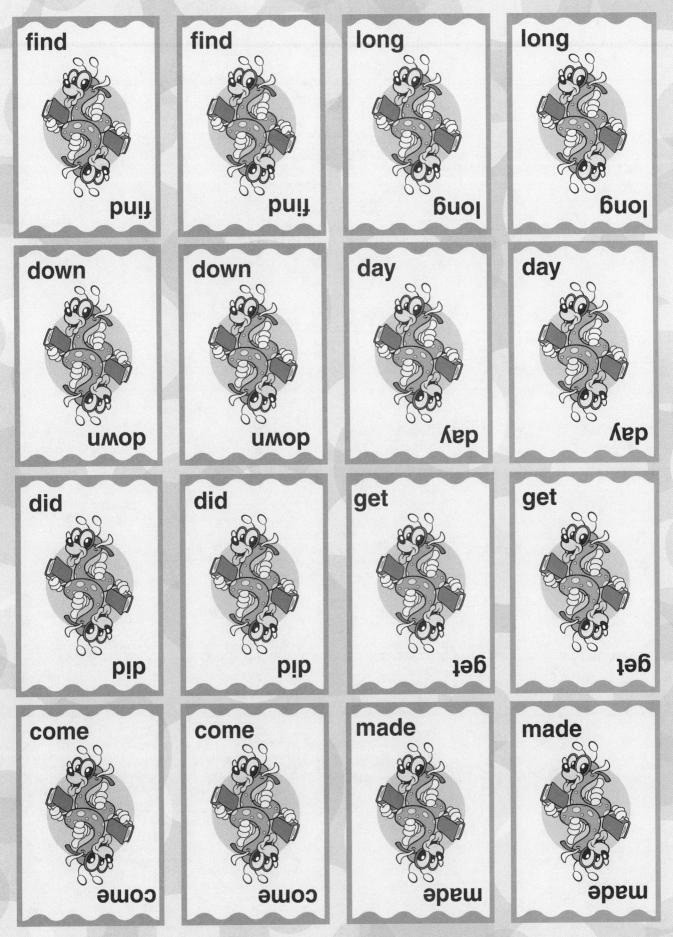

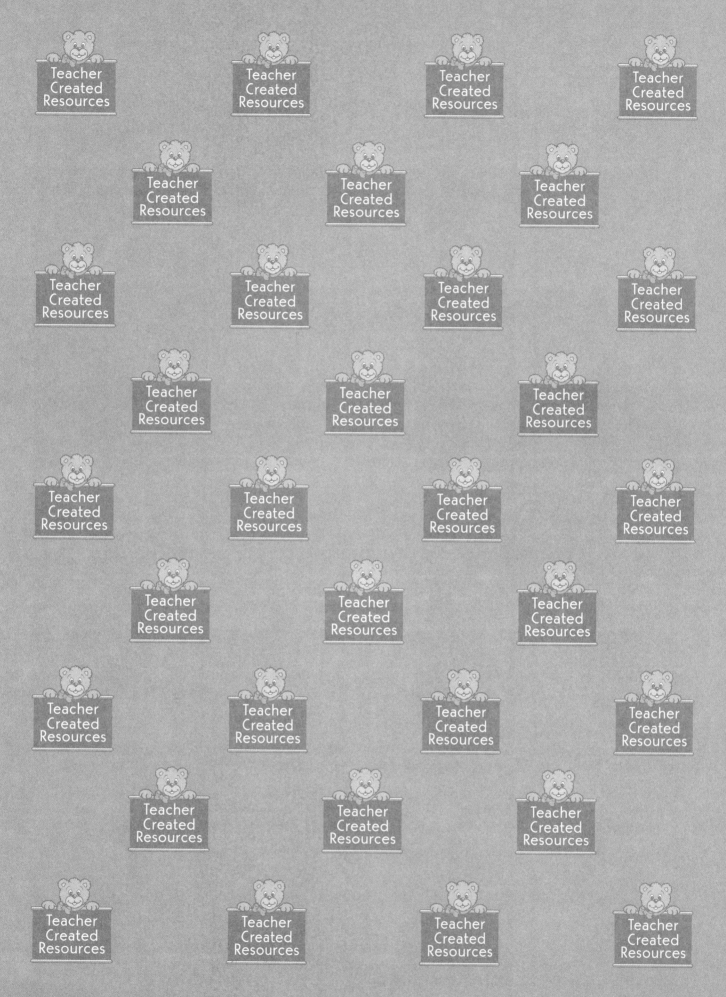

154

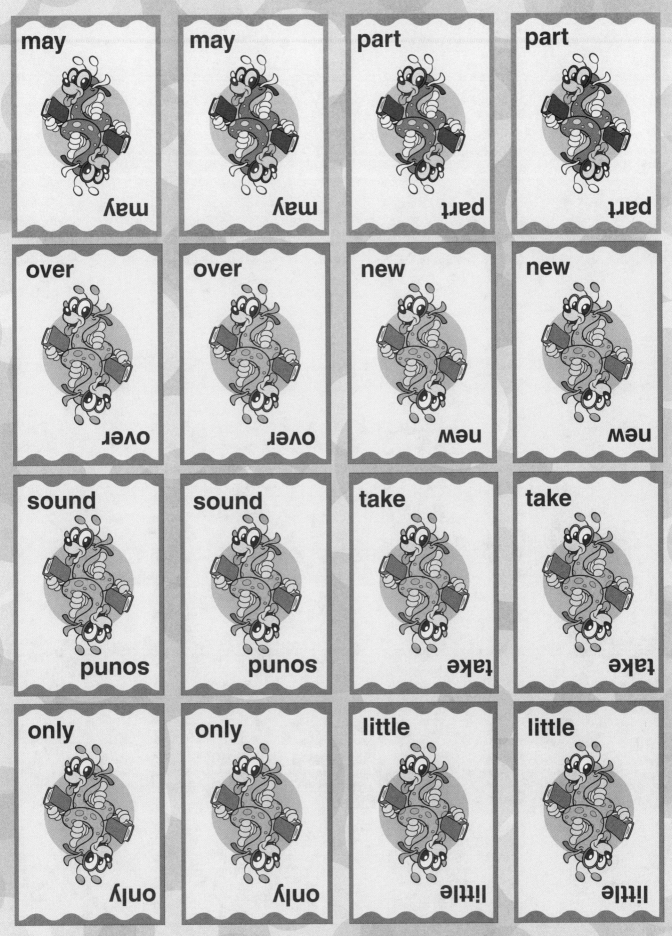

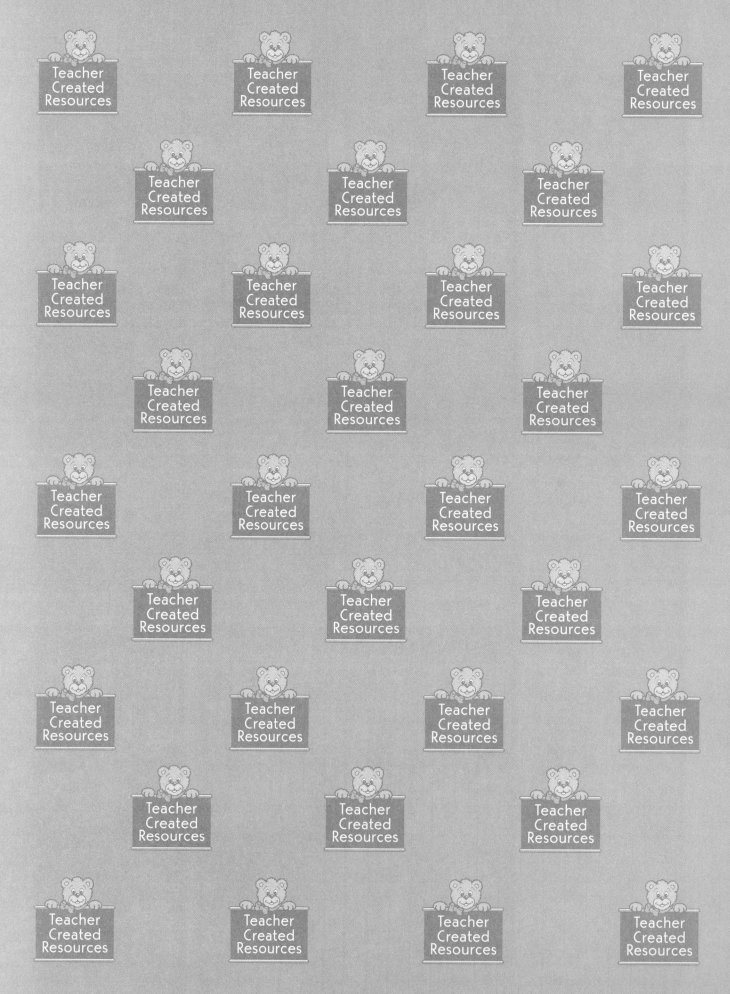

156

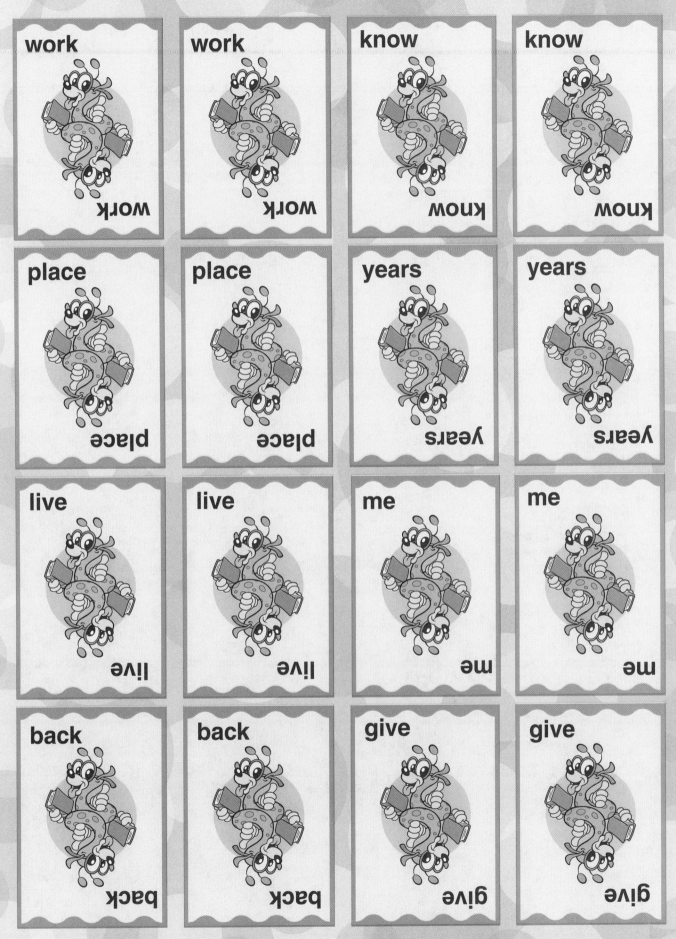

160

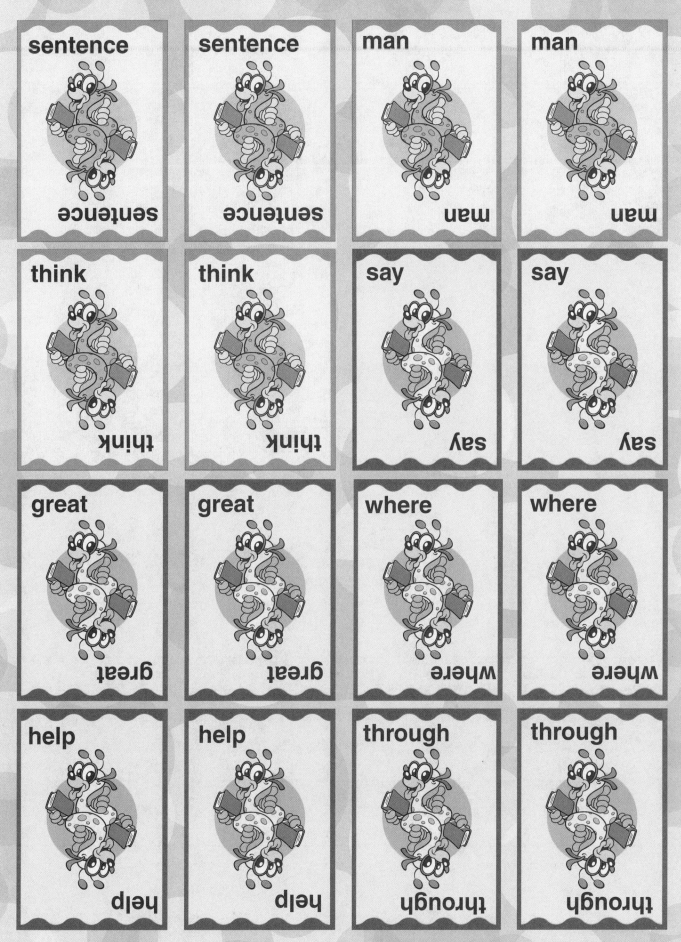

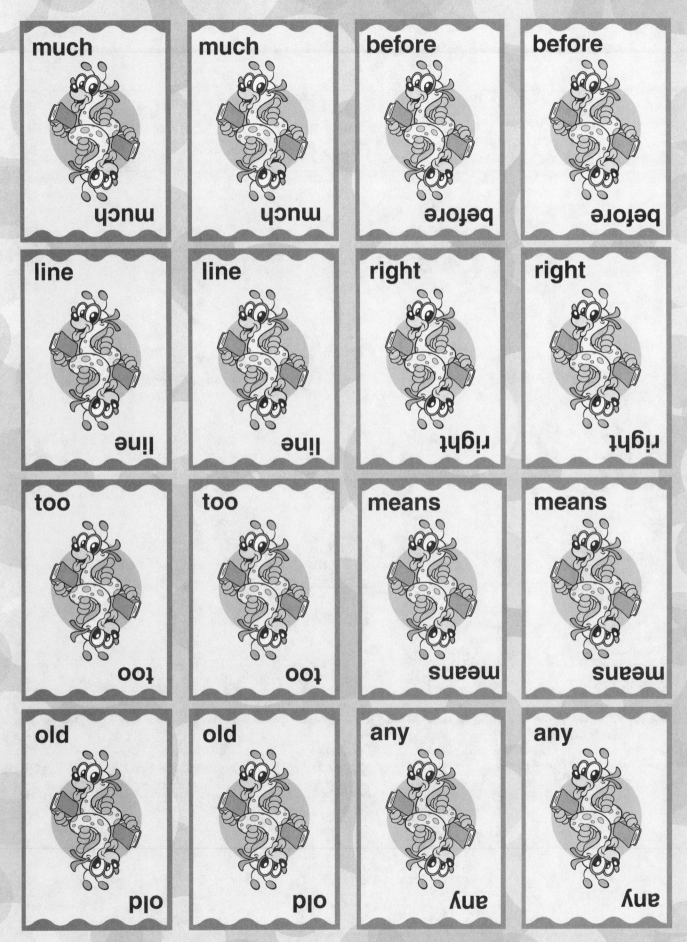

much

much

before

before

line

line

right

right

too

too

means

means

old

old

any

any

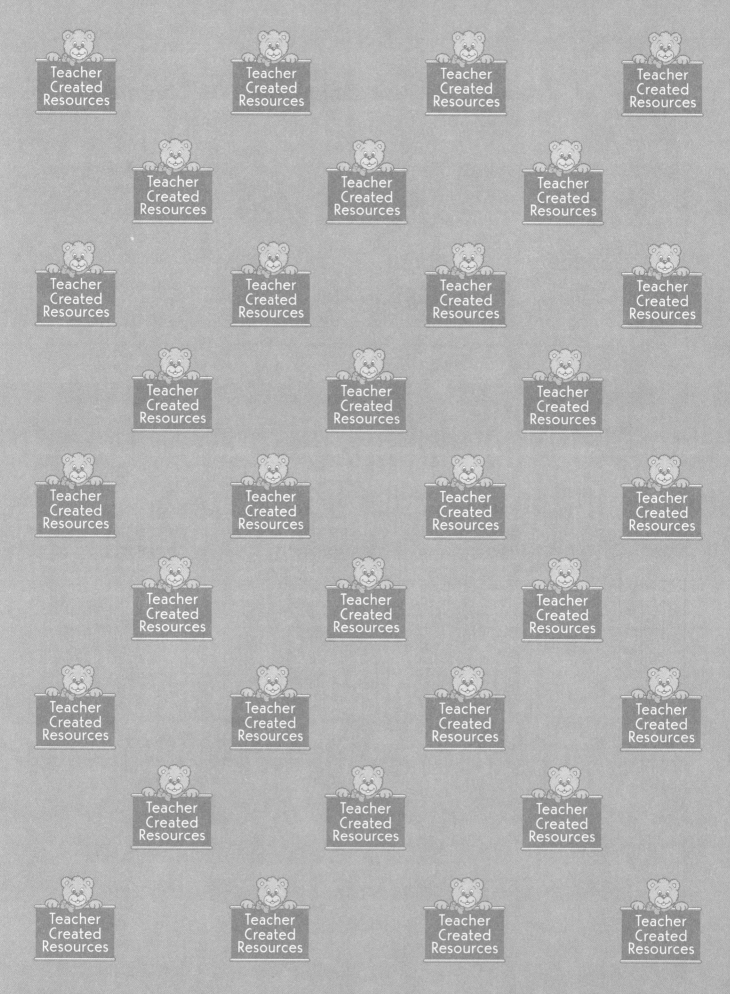

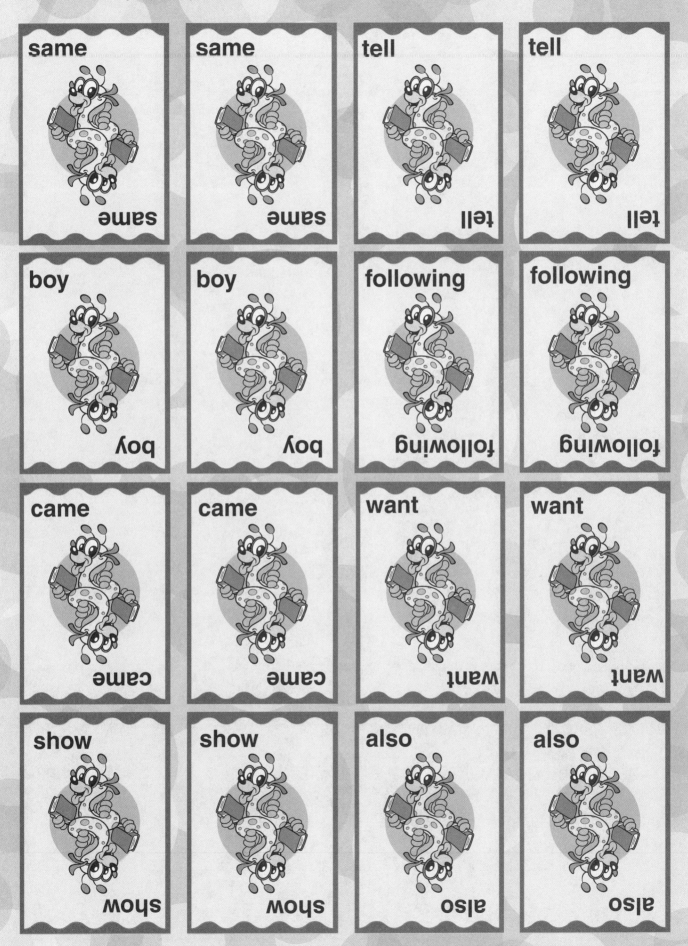

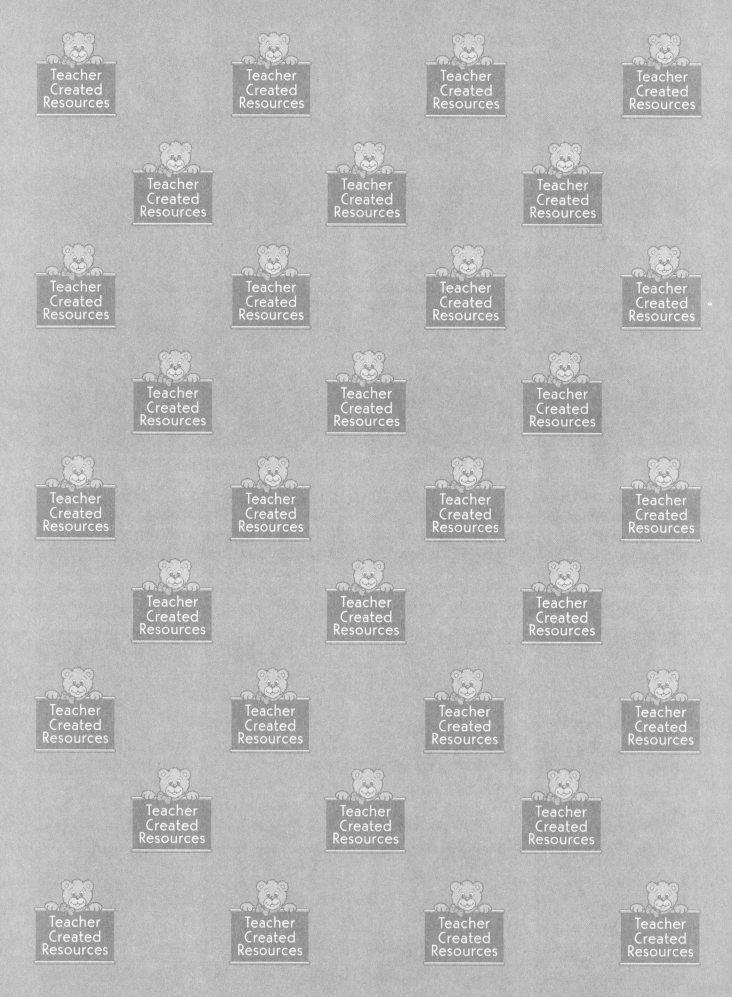

166

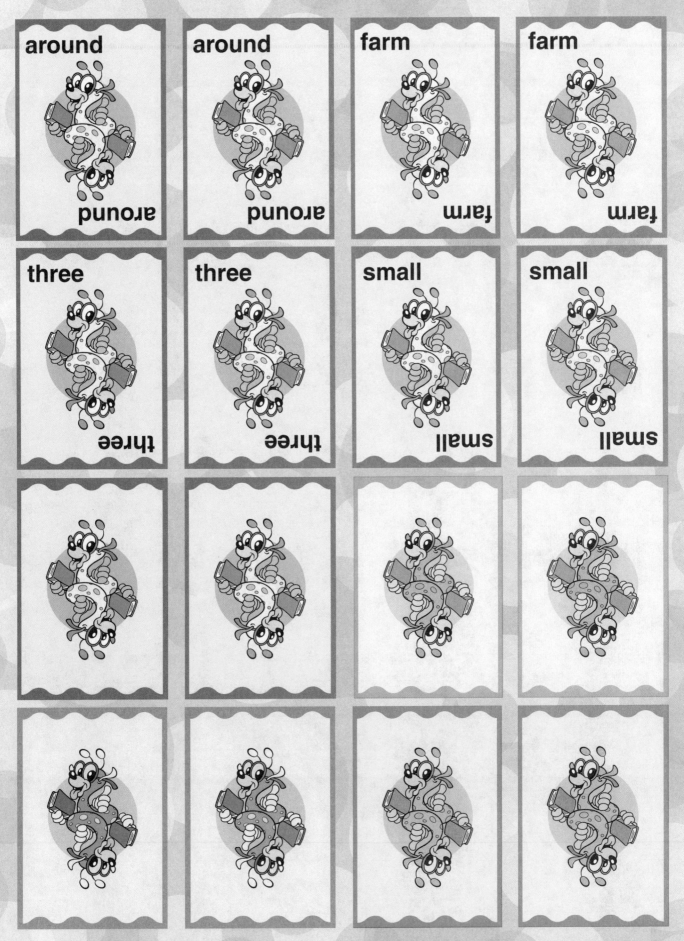

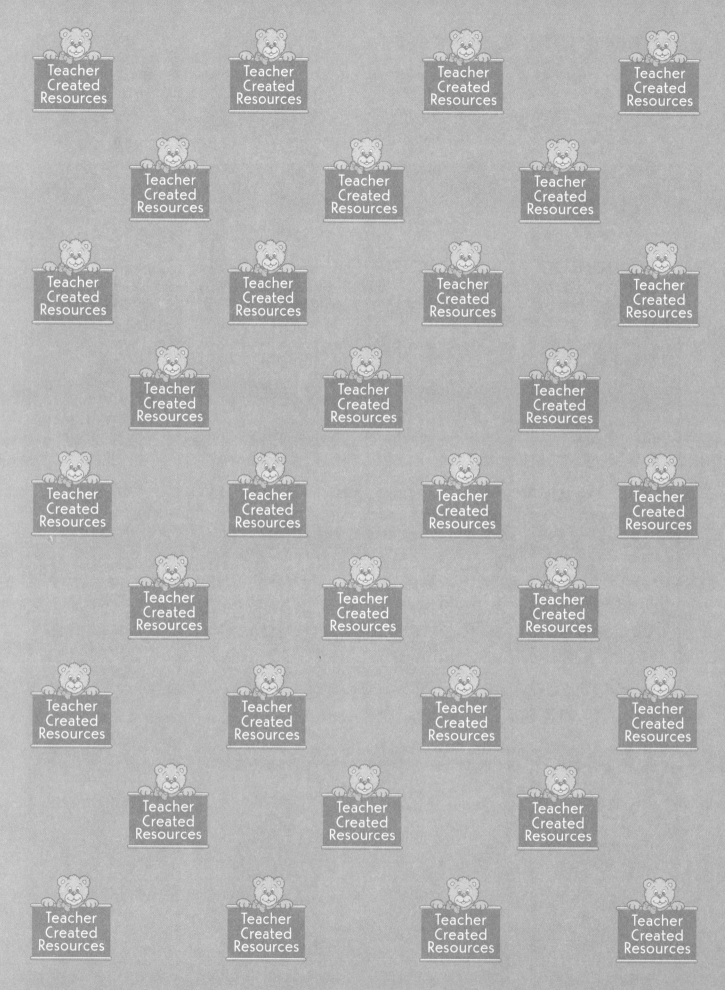

168

Reference Charts

Materials
- Picture Nouns Reference Charts (pages 171–173)
- Instant Words 51–150 Reference Chart (page 175)

Teaching Suggestions
Below are teaching suggestions for the Picture Noun and Instant Words Reference Charts.

- *Wall Charts*—Post the charts on a wall for students to use as quick and easy references.
- *Partner Reading*—Place students in pairs. Make copies of either chart and have students practice reading the words to their partners.
- *Picture Noun Reading Practice*—Use a blank piece of paper or strip of paper to cover the pictures. Have the student try to read one word at a time. To find out if he or she read it correctly, slip the paper down just one line to expose the picture. This exercise provides instant feedback, motivation, and self-teaching.
- *Picture Noun Writing Practice*—Use a blank piece of paper or strip of paper to cover the words. Have the student try to write the word for each picture one at a time. To find out if he or she wrote it correctly, slip the paper down just one line to expose the word. This exercise provides instant feedback, motivation, and self-teaching.
- *Oral Spelling Practice*—Place students in pairs. Have one student read the word from the chart while the other student tries to spell the word.
- *Independent Spelling Practice*—Use the worksheet on page 170. Have students name the picture on the worksheet and then try to write the word. Have them check their answers by looking at the Picture Noun chart. (*Note:* For beginning writers and readers, you may choose to have students do only a few words each day.)
- *Creating Phrases and Sentences*—Have students write sentences using the words on the charts.
- *Sentence Building*—Make multiple copies of the charts and hand them out to students. Have them cut out the words and make sentences or phrases. Have students paste their sentences or phrases onto a sheet of paper and take them home to read to their parents.
- *Centers*—Post the charts in centers and create your own activities.
- *Home Practice*—Send copies of the charts home for students to practice reading the words to their parents.

My Picture Noun Words

Name: _____ **Date:** _____

Directions: Write the word for each picture.

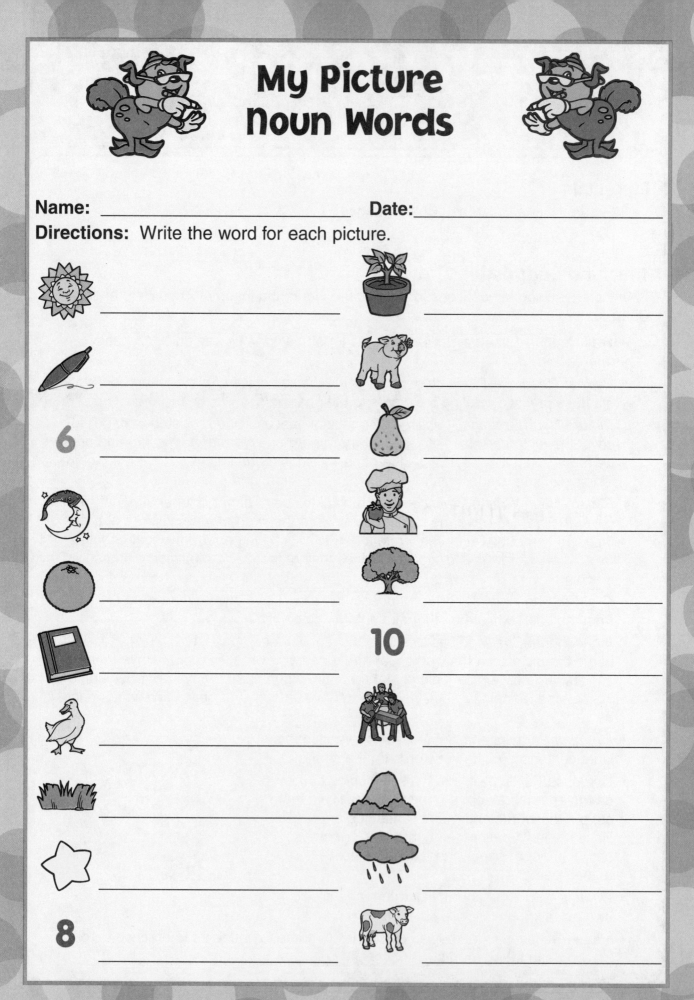

_____

_____

6 _____

_____

_____

_____

_____

_____

8 _____

_____

_____

_____

_____

_____

10 _____

_____

_____

_____

_____

Picture nouns

678 Numbers 6-10
- **6** six
- **7** seven
- **8** eight
- **9** nine
- **10** ten

Plants
- bush
- flower
- grass
- plant
- tree

Fruit
- fruit
- orange
- grape
- pear
- banana

Sky Things
- sun
- moon
- star
- cloud
- rain

Earth Things
- lake
- rock
- dirt
- field
- hill

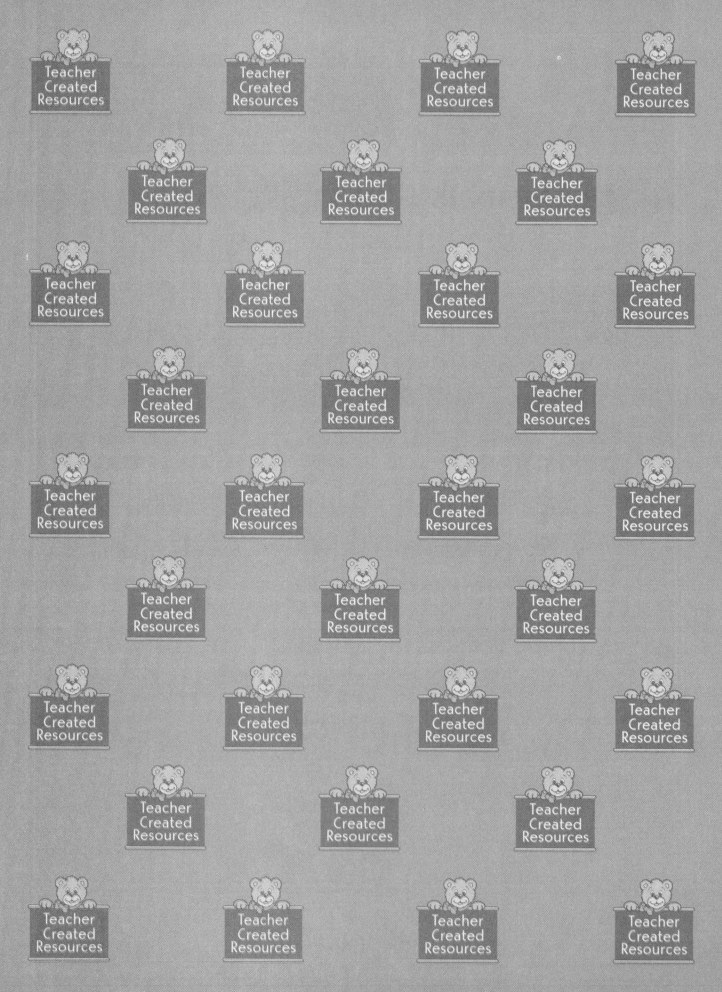

172

Picture Nouns

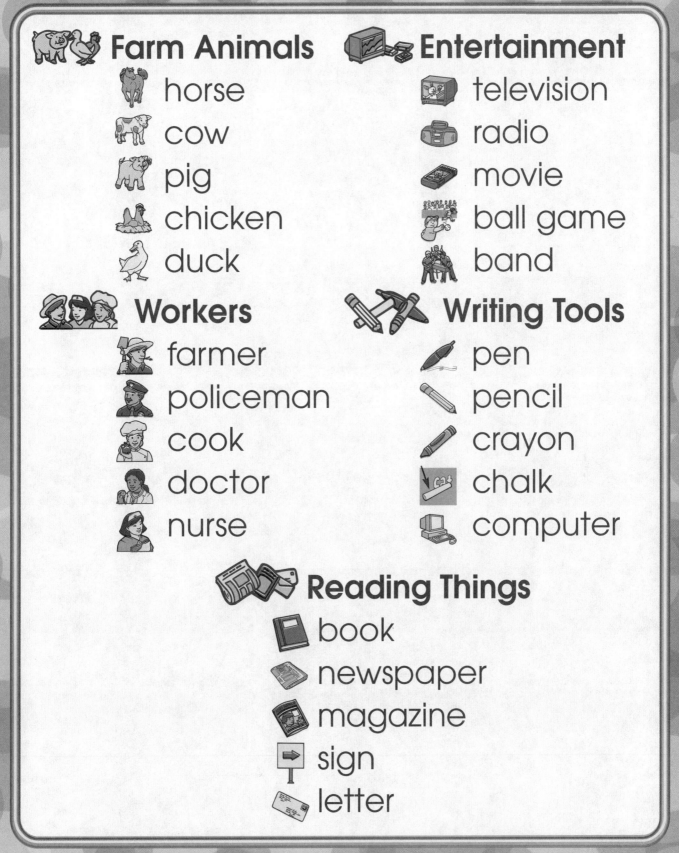

Farm Animals
- horse
- cow
- pig
- chicken
- duck

Entertainment
- television
- radio
- movie
- ball game
- band

Workers
- farmer
- policeman
- cook
- doctor
- nurse

Writing Tools
- pen
- pencil
- crayon
- chalk
- computer

Reading Things
- book
- newspaper
- magazine
- sign
- letter

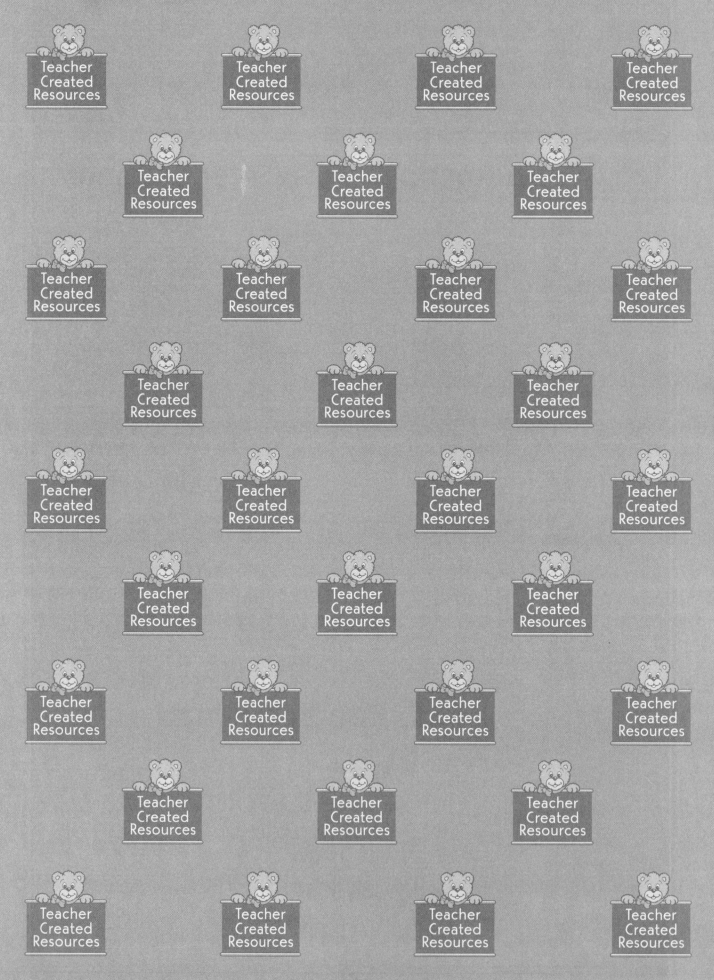

174

Instant Words 51–150

51. will	76. number	101. over	126. say
52. up	77. no	102. new	127. great
53. other	78. way	103. sound	128. where
54. about	79. could	104. take	129. help
55. out	80. people	105. only	130. through
56. many	81. my	106. little	131. much
57. then	82. than	107. work	132. before
58. them	83. first	108. know	133. line
59. these	84. water	109. place	134. right
60. so	85. been	110. years	135. too
61. some	86. called	111. live	136. means
62. her	87. who	112. me	137. old
63. would	88. am	113. back	138. any
64. make	89. its	114. give	139. same
65. like	90. now	115. most	140. tell
66. him	91. find	116. very	141. boy
67. into	92. long	117. after	142. following
68. time	93. down	118. things	143. came
69. has	94. day	119. our	144. want
70. look	95. did	120. just	145. show
71. two	96. get	121. name	146. also
72. more	97. come	122. good	147. around
73. write	98. made	123. sentence	148. farm
74. go	99. may	124. man	149. three
75. see	100. part	125. think	150. small

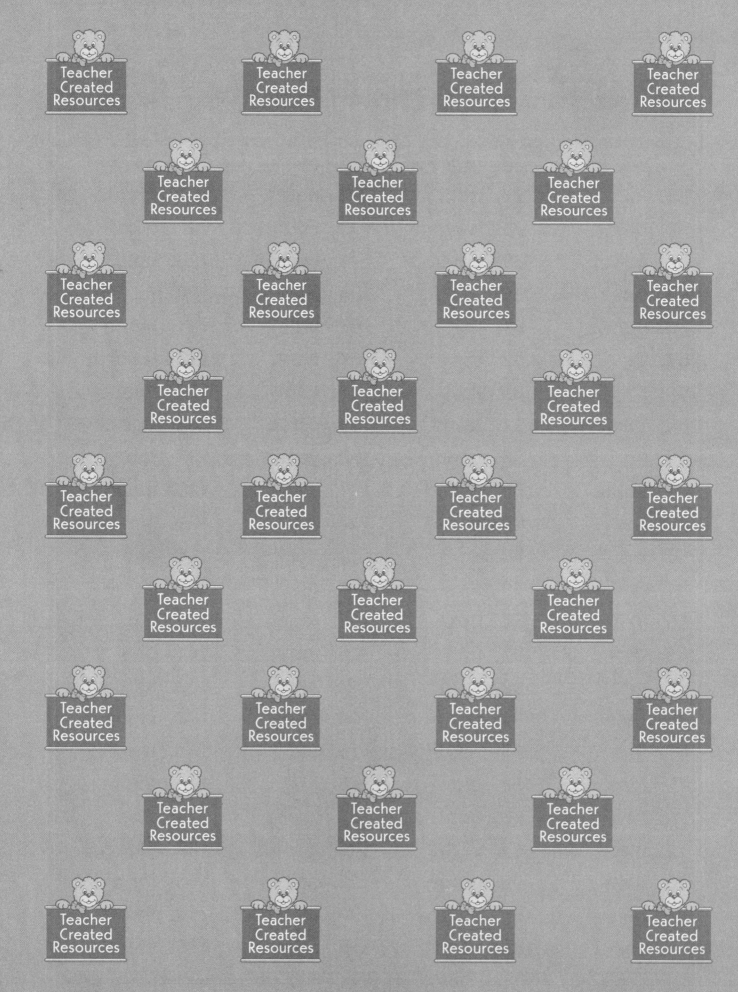